Sorrel Wilby, adventurer, author
her travels in 1981 with a trip a
drive. Since then she has cycled 17,000 kilometres through Japan,
Korea, Taiwan, China and Thailand, cycled up Japan's Mount Fuji
and along the Great Wall of China, trekked 3,000 kilometres
across Tibet, and climbed to 500 metres on Everest as the official
photojournalist for the Bicentennial Expedition team.

In 1986 Sorrel received the *Australian Geographic* Award for
excellence for extending the Australian spirit of adventure to
remote corners of the world, and in 1988 she was honoured at the
National Geographic Centenary Dinner. She was the first Australian woman to be elected as a Fellow of the internationally
renowned Explorers Club.

Sorrel is the author of the bestsellers *Tibet*, an account of her solo
trek across that mysterious land, and *Across The Top*, the story of
her traverse of the Himalaya, as well as two children's books,
Wombat and Emu Journey to Japan and *Wombat and Emu Trekking in Tibet*. She is currently travelling around Australia researching her next book, *Dreaming in Circles*.

Also by Sorrel Wilby in Sun

ACROSS THE TOP:
The World's First Complete Traverse of The Himalaya

AFRICA

a timeless soul

Sorrel Wilby

Sun
Pan Macmillan Australia

First published 1995 in Sun by Pan Macmillan Australia Pty Limited
St. Martins Tower, 31 Market Street, Sydney

Copyright © Sorrel Wilby 1995

National Library of Australia
cataloguing-in-publication data:
Wilby, Sorrel.
Africa: a timeless soul.
ISBN 0 7251 0744 8.
1. Wilby, Sorrel–Journeys–Africa. 2. Africa–
Description and travel. I. Title.
916.04329

Typeset in 11/15 Sabon by Midland Typesetters, Maryborough, Victoria
Printed by Australian Print Group, Maryborough, Vic.

For Rosanna,
who shared our dream and helped make it a reality . . .
Thank you for your vision and friendship.

CONTENTS

Acknowledgments   ix

Prologue   xv

1 MIDNIGHT AT THE OASIS   1

2 THE MARRAKESH EXPRESS   23

3 LESOTHO—KINGDOM IN THE SKY   45

4 IDI AMIN AND THE MOUNTAINS OF THE MOON   69

5 HOME OF THE MAASAI, LAND OF THE BRAVE   103

6 MOUNT KENYA AND THE AVENUE OF VOLCANOS   135

7 KILIMANJARO   151

8 HIGH IN THE ETHIOPIAN SIMIENS   173

   EPILOGUE   197

ACKNOWLEDGMENTS

In late October, 1992, Sorrel was asked to speak at a conference dinner for a major computer corporation called Data General. During the course of the evening we were chatting with the Australian managing director, Phil Kerrigan, and his marketing manager Rosanna Cordova about our plans for the future. Sorrel's book on our Himalayan traverse, *Across the Top*, was just about to be released and she had just that day finished writing up the proposal for our African venture.

Questions started getting pretty specific, but Sorrel was too nervous about the speech she was five minutes off making to realise where they were leading. The penny dropped just as she rose to begin . . .

The Managing Director wanted to back our African Expedition, but only if Rosanna could find a way to utilise the corporation's involvement through some brilliant marketing campaign.

This all came to fruition over the following weeks and on December 10—our wedding anniversary—Rosanna rang to say that Data General had agreed to be our major financial sponsor.

An incredible amount of work went into the realisation of Rosanna's marketing campaign, and for every hour Sorrel and I spent climbing a mountain, Rosanna and her team of helpers clocked up three or four compiling a magificent album of our images and words. This was distributed to 150 key clients who shared our adventure as it unfolded through regular updates and postcards.

We had a fantastic time working with the Data General team and their commitment to us went way beyond the normal 'call of duty'. They almost became family, and Sorrel and I will always be indebted to them for their support—thanks to you all, financial and otherwise. A thousand thankyous from the top of the mountains and the bottom of our hearts.

For our very comfortable flights around Africa and home to Australia we wish to thank John Murray and Joe Hanson from South African Airways. SAA also cargoed our 150 kg of dried foods and equipment to Kenya—which all arrived on time and intact. Thanks to our friends Ian MacIntosh and Laurence and Jo McManus for helping to coordinate that one!

Once again we were lucky to have our soles (and souls!) well supported by Hi-Tec Boots. Thanks, Trevor—you are one in a zillion and we love you heaps. Thanks also to Hi-Tec South Africa and Judith Drake and family for on-ground and logistic support.

As always we carried our gear in Macpac Backpacks and slept well protected inside a Macpac tent. Their Wilderness range of clothing just gets better and better, so to Bruce, Dan, Fraser and all the team in New Zealand, a big thanks from Loretta and JoJo for constantly finding new ways to improve on perfection.

All our drinking water was filtered through a Katadyn water filter, which is probably why we were never badly affected by nasties; pretty amazing for eight months in Africa, eh? Thanks,

Greg. Thanks also to Paddy Pallins for supplying us with all our climbing equipment and Grant Minervini Agencies for all those other vital bits and pieces, especially the MSR stove.

Our thanks to Olympus (R. Gunz Pty Ltd) for cameras and lenses that never die no matter how many times you accidentally launch them into space from a mountain top, and to Jonathon Bays from Eveready for taking care of our battery needs again.

To Ian Day for supplying us with Cerola toasted apricot muesli, to Bettina Bezzina of Maxwell House Coffee and Cottee's drinks fame, to Continental for their Cup-a-Soups, dried vegies and pasta and sauce dishes, and Sun Valley True Fruits for fruit leather and carob bars—thank you again for continuing your culinary support. A special thanks to our friends Ted and Sue Walker from our local Ulladulla Go-Vita health food store for weighing, mixing, packing and donating eights months' worth of dried fruit and nut lunches.

For extra B-B-Bounce, Sorrel and I take multi-vitamins and Beroccas, kindly supplied by Roche Australia. They also kept us alive with Aquasun UV protection products and Lariam anti-malaria tablets. Wellcome took care of our other medicinal needs.

Thanks to Steve Raine, manager of OPSM at Batemans Bay, who gave us groovy Bolle sunglasses and binoculars so we could spot rare Wallia ibex and the like. Thanks to John Broons of Smiths Timber for his generous support as well.

In Africa we'd like to thank—first and foremost—Paul and Susan Cameron, now ex-Australian High Commission in Nairobi, who were so kind and hospitable to Sorrel and me, and especially to Paul for the bruises I received in the back of his Suzuki 4WD. Thanks also to Glen and Diana and the rest of the staff at the Commission for their support and friendship. Iian Allan from Tropical Ice in Nairobi helped greatly with ground support and local knowledge for East Africa. If you ever want to climb Mount Kenya or go on a safari in style, this is the man to do it with.

Mick and Di Jones of Lesotho Pony Trekking went out of their way to make our trek and stay in Lesotho special and all the staff of Imzilen Brothers in Morocco did the same for us there. To Michael and Jocelyn Wilson—two wonderful friends who looked after us during our stopovers in London, thanks for opening your hearts and home to us, and to Catherine Oddie, Robert Olo-imooja ole Rerente and their special Maasai family in the Loita Hills—likewise.

Finally, thanks to John and Sue Kasoulis at the Arcadia Twin Cinema, Ulladulla, for keeping my job for me, to Sorrel's Mum and Dad for keeping our affairs in order while we were away and last (but by no means least) special thanks to the best authors' management service/literary agent in the whole wide world, Selwa Anthony.

Chris Ciantar
August, 1994

Africa amongst the continents will teach it to you:
that God and the Devil are one,
the majesty co-eternal . . .

KAREN BLIXEN, *OUT OF AFRICA.*

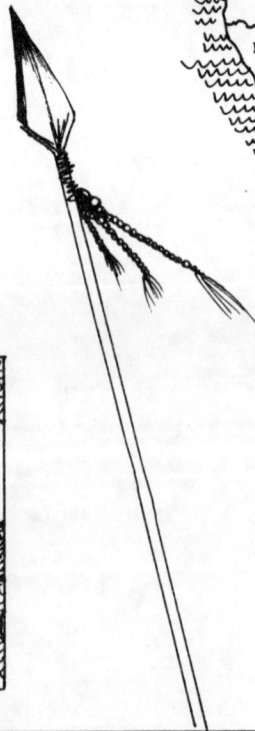

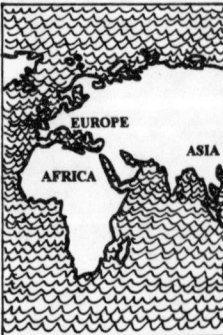

PROLOGUE

'The sun has bled all colour from the world. The earth has turned to dust. The air around me is motionless. Time and space are one.

It must be at least 40 degrees out here—but who's counting? Anything over thirty-seven is unbearable without shade. Without water.

I stand transfixed. As static as the thorn trees, as silent as a stone. It's like being inside an over-exposed photograph. Lifeless. Two-dimensional.

Two figures appear on the horizon to my left; a sudden flash of brilliant red. They are an image, swimming through emulsion, floating into focus ... into being. They flow, as liquid, through the heat haze towards me.

They are tall. Proud. Unmistakably Maasai.

They move closer. I can make out the long spears they carry across their shoulders ... the wooden 'rungus' in their hands.

Their heads are shaved and coloured with ochre and their elegant necks are collared with beads. Their earlobes are pierced, distended and flapping. Their legs are hairless and sleek. They do not seem to sweat.

They stop briefly to greet me then disappear—as unaccountably as they have come.

Long after they have gone, I can still feel my heart beat. I can still smell their courage. They have left so much more than footprints in the sand ...

Is that the heat now, throbbing in my temples? The pulse of Africa rising in my blood? The drum beat of a thousand hooves can quake the soil beneath me, but nothing moves me quite like beauty.

Oh, Africa ... if this is love, then tell me, at what moment did I cease to resist you? At what point did your clichéd illusion become a sincere truth? The florid text of guide books ... the oversells on film ... they promised to uplift me; they prophesied new life. But I doubted I could find it here—not in this Godforsaken age. Not on this unholy void. Yet here you are, in all your brutish glory, breathing magic into my lungs ... again. Quenching this thirsty soul of mine with your bewitching charm.'

I must confess from the outset that my expectations of this continent were never high. I did not go there to be wooed. It was Chris's idea entirely, and not for a moment did I think I would adore it. Indeed, I doubted I could be at peace in any realm outside my beloved Himalaya. I really thought I'd left my heart up there, just one small step from heaven.

I had always known—even before I first set foot in Nepal—where I stood in relation to her marvellous peaks and remarkable people. I had always known that land to have a soul. That land had been a part of me, long, long before I was even born.

But of Africa ... I could not say. I did not know, intuitively, and in a way I didn't even want to find out. If I loved it, as everyone insisted I would, would it not be like having a second child? Would I not compare it, constantly, to the first? Love both less perhaps, for the need to be fair?

Africa was, after all, a paradox, and my reaction to it was the same.

The myth, the romance of Africa, was alive and well in my mind—the endless plains, the boundless skies, and all that savage beauty held between. But so too was the truth; the ceaseless misery of Africa; the senseless civil wars, the droughts and famines, the tyrannies and carnage.

The colonial past—the era both celebrated and exploited by the Great White Hunters and brave explorers—was long dead, and for that I was both regretful and thankful. Self-government was the right of every nation; self-determination the right of every individual; but for many the dream of independence had become a nightmare of insecurity, brutality and economic collapse.

Whatever the cost of colonialism, it was nothing compared to the damage which followed. The promise of freedom was short-lived; the idealism of liberty crushed. Military dictatorships and one-party states proved just as oppressive and the continent slowly regressed. In the last decade alone incomes have fallen, hunger has increased and unemployment continues to rise. Africa's foreign debt of US$230 billion is equal to the continent's overall Gross National Product.

Overall, Africans were almost as poor—in 13 nations poorer—than they were at Independence. About a quarter of sub-Saharan Africa—more than 100 million people in all—face chronic food shortages. Ten thousand children a day still die in Africa from causes linked to malnutrition and the lack of health care.

Paradise—while not yet completely lost—clearly did not last long in this part of the world. Growing populations were hungry for land, forests were being cleared to feed that need and over-grazing rendered much of Africa's arable land barren. In 50 years, approximately 30 million square kilometres of farming land had become infertile. According to the analysts, desertification and erosion were spreading out of control; the Sahara and Kalahari were moving some 200 kilometres closer each year.

The big-game sanctuaries of the seventies were also under siege. They were no longer a refuge for wildlife—they were killing fields for the poaching gangs, backed by heinous factions of wealthy traders, unprincipled officials and greedy politicians. Several species face extinction if the illegal trade in rhino horn and ivory continues.

Where was that 'image of unbounded freedom'? Where was literature's 'escapist Utopia'? Where were Blixen's herds of elephant, pacing along as if they had an appointment at the end of the world? Where, indeed, had all the beauty, all the hope, gone?

There were many reasons to despair for Africa. On paper, in words and pictures, it was doomed. Condemned. And yet, for all that was damnable, for all that perplexed, angered and saddened me, I was still charmed by what I'd seen and read of the contrary. I could not let go of the promise completely.

Even more surely than I knew that the Himalaya had always— would always—be a part of me, I knew I was destined to travel beyond it. At the very core of my being, the music I danced to, the rhythm within me, was not the song of a particular place or location. It was the very anthem of adventure itself . . . the lilt of the unknown . . . the call of the wild.

Once *that* fire in my belly was rekindled, I had to fuel it with a vision. The vision, for better or worse, was Africa. I dwelt less and less on the crimes of despotic regimes, the fate of the rhino, the remnants of Eden, focused more and more on the Snows of Kilimanjaro and the Mountains of the Moon. By name alone these peaks awakened me, filled me with a sense of mystery and excitement. I could not resist.

For what is was worth, I had to see, hear, feel, taste and smell that immense, ancient, mysterious and terrible place myself—before it vanished completely. Before even the mountains were lost to the future. I had to see if Africa, like Nepal, possessed a heart. If it, too, retained a timeless soul.

MIDNIGHT
AT THE OASIS

I T WAS SO BIG. So monotonous. So ... empty. We were in the
air for hours, passing over it, trying to take it all in. A single
feature of the earth's surface, as large as the USA ... I had
flown over deserts before, but never had one left me feeling so
bereft. What made it worse, so much more intimidating, was the
fact that we would soon be trekking through it. Yes, trekking.
Again. Through—of all places—the infamous Sahara. Downright
miracle I wasn't divorced, really.

Africa, as I may have mentioned, was Chris's idea—but true
to form, I'd taken the nucleus of a somewhat formless notion
and cultured it into yet another masochistic, 'character-building'
epic. We were going to trek through and climb all the major
ranges and highest mountains on the entire continent. Starting
in the north, we planned to trek through the Ahaggar Mountains
in the heart of the Algerian Sahara, then tackle the High Atlas
range in Morocco. In the south we hoped to scale Thabana

Algeria

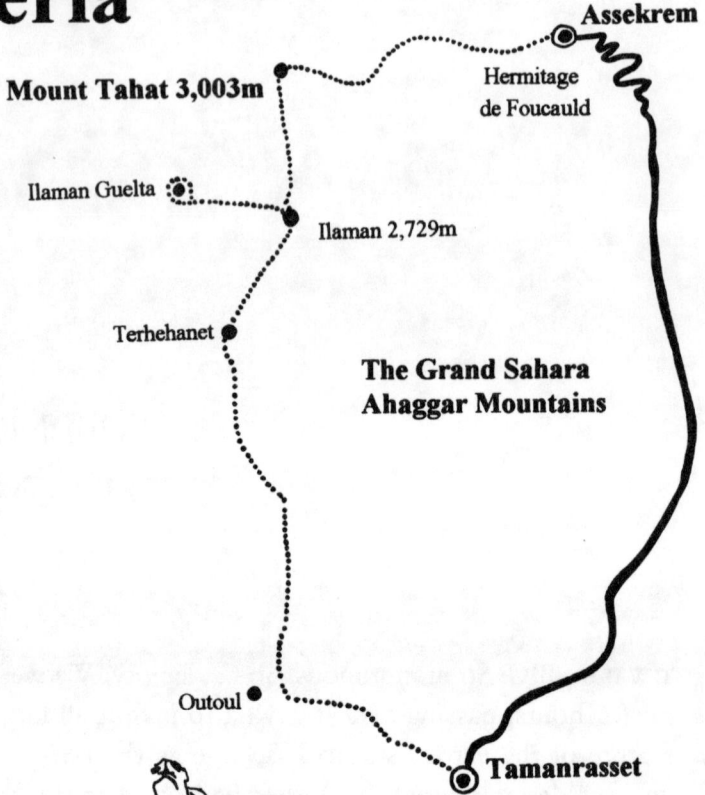

Assekrem

Mount Tahat 3,003m

Hermitage
de Foucauld

Ilaman Guelta

Ilaman 2,729m

Terhehanet

**The Grand Sahara
Ahaggar Mountains**

Outoul

Tamanrasset

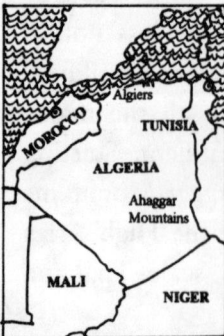

Algiers

MOROCCO
TUNISIA
ALGERIA
Ahaggar
Mountains
MALI
NIGER

Ntlenyana and explore a bit of the Drakensberg and Maluti range. The equatorial east held the bulk of Africa's high realms and there we anticipated climbing several peaks in the Rwenzoris, Mount Kenya, Kilimanjaro, an assortment of lesser volcanoes, dormant and active, and the Simien escarpment of Ethiopia. Not forgetting the final point on the old compass, we would head west and climb Mount Cameroon—the wettest place on earth. The extreme diversity of the landscapes we would encounter was absolutely staggering.

I did mention this was *Chris's* idea, didn't I?

For those of you who don't know me, I'm 'The Travelling Wilby'. My husband Chris is more often than not referred to as 'the victim'. As Charles Woolly so eloquently put it in his *60 Minutes* profile on me: 'It is hard enough just doing a story about Sorrel Wilby ... imagine what it must be like being married to her!'

To be totally honest, I'm not even worth talking to—let alone living with—unless I'm in the throes of some earth-shattering, mind-boggling adventure. Unless I'm out there, taking on the universe, I don't feel worthy of my own existence. And Chris? Well ... Chris is only happy when he's sleeping or fishing the tide. I had tricked him into including the Sahara in our African itinerary by speaking of it only in the most carefully chosen, pelagic terms: '*Ocean* of sand' had been particularly successful, and '*Sea* without water' had worked as well.

So, here we were now ... several thousand metres above it; Chris adrift in hyperspace, me awash with fear.

For all its vacancy, for all the desolation it instilled, I was completely entranced by the never-ending wasteland beneath me. The hands which shaped this vista were obviously strong ones; aggressive and powerful. The dunes were rippled whorls from massive thumbs, the escarpments knuckles of a tight, angry fist. The Spirit of Raoul, the 'Drummer of Death', was said to move with the wind across the Sahara, and from this vulturous height it was easy to see where he'd tattooed his dirge on the earth's sunburnt skin. His rhythm was relentless. It had been for two and a half million years.

I sent Chris down the back of the plane to chat with the stewards. Algeria was a Muslim country, and a friendly exchange with him would—I hoped—be less misconstrued than one with me. I was suddenly anxious to know how one went about hiring and controlling camels in the middle of nowhere with a half-forgotten repertoire from the do-it-yourself manual: 'French in Ten Minutes a Day'.

When I first met Chris, he had recently returned from one of his Hilton holidays in Europe and his preparatory attempts to master this foreign tongue were still visible throughout the interior of his Corona: 'LE ASHTRAY', 'LE STEERING WHEEL' and 'VOILA! LE GLOVE-BOX AVEC TOLL COUPONS!' were each neatly labelled. Camels did not, admittedly, have door handles, but I trusted his vocabulary extended beyond the vehicular.

We had spent very little time researching the practicalities of our climbs prior to our apt April Fool's Day departure. It seemed every waking moment (and many unconscious ones) had been spent preparing physically and financially for the expedition. An anthropologically inclined girlfriend had helped me compile a substantial set of notes on the various cultures we were likely to encounter *en route*, but actual 'nuts and bolts' information was lacking. The best we could come up with in the limited time available was a photocopied map and overview of each country from the *Encyclopaedia Britannica*, a short stack of related but outdated *National Geographic* articles and a wad of rather disappointing 'Consular Travel Advices' from the Department of Foreign Affairs and Trade in Canberra. Nearly every one they'd issued recommended that Australians avoid travelling to the country in question until further notice. Some of them were back-dated several months, others several years. God, in his infinite wisdom, had placed most of the mountains of Africa in places where deteriorating security and continuous states of emergency were rife.

In the last-minute packing frenzy, we'd overlooked the need to include—among other things (such as bullet-proof vests and a collection of amulets)—a French-English dictionary. Two days in Algiers had left us feeling frustrated and sorry for the oversight, and the prospect of spending several weeks without one in the desert now upon us was not at all inspired.

I was half-expecting Chris to return from the rear galley with a black eye. It was easy to make mistakes with the rudiments of any language and easy for an artless question to become—in the confusion of tense and pronunciation—an unseemly insult. He was bound to call someone a camel's arse instead of asking how one was kicked.

But Chris returned triumphant. The steward had spoken English. He had a friend who was a vet, who had a friend who had a camel. He had pencilled his name and that of a reputable travel agent in Tamanrasset on the back of a napkin. No addresses; just the names. Great! All we had to do was stand in the middle of the street and cry 'Mohammed!'—twice—and hope either of the right ones came to our rescue. It would be a bit like picking the right 'Smith' at random from the phone book.

Momentarily distracted by the scrawl on the serviette and without landmarks or visual clues to suggest where we were in relation to the ground, I was surprised to suddenly find the pilot halfway through his landing procedure. After 2000 kilometres of nothingness, I was unprepared for my first close-up view of the 'lesser' Ahaggar Mountains. There they were; just a stone's throw from the tarmac: an exhibit of failed experiments from the bakeries of hell. Great high-domed loaves of sunbaked rock, half a dozen massive scones, a couple of sad soufflés and a bread stick, haphazardly arranged for judgment on the desert floor.

The devil had his fan-forced oven turned up high, but his culinary creations would continue to defy the blasting heat. They were as hard as fired terracotta already, impervious to all but the most persistent, vicious wind.

At 1000 metres the Spirit of Raoul began to buffet his baleful welcome, using the plane for a drum. The seat belt light was flashing and the chief flight attendant was invoking the Will of Allah through the intercom. The turbulence was terrifying, especially for someone like me, with an over-developed penchant for motion sickness and a phobia for flying. We were being tossed all over the place, like an autumn leaf in a hurricane. I would have closed my eyes, but I couldn't take them off all the other aircraft lining the runway. At least four of them were upside down. The others had just been blown off course. The sense of *déjà vu* I experienced was completely overwhelming.

We touched down safely, albeit slightly askew. The forward-cabin rows of French tourists clapped. I usually found this European tradition absurd, as if landing a plane was a matter of chance or a special performance beyond the pilot's normal range of aerial exploits, but in this case it did seem appropriate. I would have joined them actually, but I was having some trouble dislodging my clawed hands from the armrests of the seat.

Once out of the terminal, reunited with our hefty duffle bags, we joined a long queue for taxis. The French package-tour group were whisked away in a special fleet of gleaming four-wheel drives, so the line-up was prodominantly local.

There was only one place to go from this airport: Tamanrasset. The capital and main administrative hub of Le Grand Sud, 12 kilometres further south. The one and only gateway to the first of our mountain-based adventures!

Before long, a couple of bright yellow battered Land Cruisers appeared in a cloud of dust, screeching to a halt at no point in particular alongside the kerb. Years had passed since I'd witnessed a *melée* like that which ensued among the hot, disorderly throng, spilling into the gutter like so much overflow from a Vinnies clothing bin. Local veiled tribesmen, visiting businessmen, a frail white missionary and an army of rotund Islamic bag ladies all tried to mount the two vehicles at once. All but for six-a-piece failed.

The rules which one usually took for granted in queues did not apply here. It was a bloody free-for-all.

Chris and I weren't in any hurry. It was safer, and far more fun, to watch the fracas than become a part of it. Since there was so little difference between some fully swathed passengers and their Gargantuan bundles of bound belongings, the driver's assistants occasionally made the mistake of throwing baggage in the hold and people on the roof. Objections to such rough treatment invariably led to a fuselage of abuse.

After an hour, our moment came. Looking very much like a desert version of Jed Clampet's well-loaded jalopy, we bounded—at 120 kilometres an hour—towards the city. Granny had been superseded on the luggage-racks by a two-metre Tuareg in a pale blue calf-length shirt and pantaloons. Our duffle bags formed a sort of bobsled around him and the loose end of the bolt of white fabric he had wound around his head and face made a great windsock.

From first impressions, the indigenous Tuareg[1] were a noble people; dignified, aloof, arcane. Despite military defeat by the French in the early 1920s, they had retained an air of invincibility about them. The menfolk were very tall, with average height of six feet (183 cm), and lean and lanky. Their turban-like veils and preference for badly dyed indigo cloth (which invariably left their skins tinged with blue) were legendary. They were so physically striking in this garb, the fact that they had become a minority in their own home town was not immediately apparent. Like Sikhs in an Indian community, they stood out in a crowd and gave an overall impression of supremacy and dominance.

We checked into the fetid but affordable Hotel Tinhinane on

[1] Derived from the Arabic word *tarek*, meaning 'abandoned by God'. The name was given to them by Arab invaders—who were somewhat unimpressed by their pagan ways—during the Middle Ages.

the main street, then set off to find Mohammed the travel agent and/or Mohammed the camel trader.

For a city of 100 000 people, Tam[2] was pretty laid-back. On a holiday, during the hottest part of the day, it was virtually comatose. Everything bar the cafes was shut. These were not in short supply though, as nearly every second commercial venture in the tourism-oriented hub of town served coffee and Coca-Cola.

With the search for Mohammed et Mohammed over before it had even begun, we bought some bottled spring water—the on-tap stuff was both dubious in quality and supply—and sat down at one of several trestle tables set up on the footpath. It was hard to tell which outdoor furniture belonged to each particular establishment since they all kind of ran into one another. We were moved twice before we got it right.

The dusty avenue of trees for which this town was famed afforded us a little shade from what was still, despite the advantage of a relatively high altitude, an oppressive Saharan heat. Since we were being completely ignored by the other tourists sitting near us, we looked beyond them to the street itself to get a better feel for where we were.

The rough concrete single-storey buildings around us were painted a uniform pinkish rust colour; echoing the hue of desert dunes at dusk. The doorways were bordered in stark white wash, as were the bases of each tree to thigh-height. Foliage came in the form of postcard selections, nailed in steel racks to the tree trunks at eye-level. Beneath them hawkers sold single cigarettes from a variety of packets, displayed in wooden attachés. The odd souvenir shop was readily discernible by its 'awning' of carpets, prayer rugs, saddle cloths and *bric-à-brac* hanging from a frame above its entrance. The whole effect was quite lovely—but it didn't exactly cause my heart to skip a beat. With a provocative name like Tamanrasset, I had hoped for more, but this was no

---

[2] The 'street-wise' abbreviation by which overlanders and Sahara trekkers refer to Tamanrasset.

North African Kathmandu, no matter how much imagination you had to play with. There would be no goats emerging from taxis here, no rickshaws full of bleeding offal, and not a single 'Sincere Supermarket Centre' or 'Humane Fit' tailor anywhere. Tam's heyday was well and truly over. Even the ghosts of times past— the camel caravans bearing gold, ivory, salt and slaves—had left for lack of interest.

Traffic—on this day— was virtually non-existent. A couple of cars with wild-looking drivers, and a single camel, passed by, the latter *en route* to the local *patisserie*. The aristocratic-looking rider brought his beast to a standstill by tugging on a nose rope and planting a bare heel in the camel's shoulder. He dismounted, swinging off an ornamental three-pronged pommel, purchased a croissant, then rode off into the shimmering blue distance. The vision was as close to quirky as this place would probably ever get.

As the daylight hours slowly melted away, a few of the travel agencies in town opened. We resumed our search for the elusive Mohammeds. We didn't find either of *the* Mohammeds, but we did find *a* Mohammed, a helpful bloke with not more than a dozen words of English to his credit—which was surprisingly more than anyone else had in these parts. This is not an arrogant criticism, rather an indication of how frustrating it was being a dumb monolingual Australian in a totally unfamiliar place.

The 12 words were good ones, though—absolutely imperative for survival in a desert and, coupled with Chris's meagre offerings (incongruously, he also knew how to say the word for 'rain' in Arabic!) and my own slow recall of high-school *spreken de French*, we were set like the proverbial jelly. We hadn't found our camel, but at least we knew how to ask for one now. We also knew how to ask for water, how to say 'The pen is on the table' and how to introduce ourselves and say please and thank you. We also knew how to say, 'How much? You must be *craaazy!*'

which, in an economy currently exploiting tourism to the max, was most important of all.

The next day was Friday, another holiday by virtue of the normal Muslim week. It was like Sunday is to Christians. Some tourist-related facilities were open, however, and using our newly aquired command of the language—not to mention the fortuitous arrival on the scene of one very wind-burnt, deeply tanned bilingual tour chaperon named Crystal—we were home and hosed within the hour.

The Tuareg chosen to accompany us into the Ahaggar was one Monsieur Intakarnet. All I could see of him on our first meeting were his two tiny rheumy eyes peering through the narrow slit of his *tougoulmust*,[3] and the fine-boned but leathery hands he placed inside my own great paws in greeting. His fingernails were bright pink and twinkled like a set of rose quartz stones upon my palms. He wasn't much over five feet (155 cm) tall—just knee-high to a *sauterelle* as far as Tuaregs go.

I guessed he was in his fifties. He was born in the desert, would die in the desert and knew every track, rise and pebble within it as well as he knew the lines, mounts and marks of his own hands. Together they mapped the story of his life.

He would use not one but three camels to bear our goods and chattels through the wilderness. Wow! Throw in some frankincense and myrrh, a star and a couple more of those flowing robes and we'd be the closest thing to a living Christmas card this side of Bethlehem!

Camels do not come cheap in the desert, but we negotiated a mutually agreeable deal, worked out an itinerary and even added to our list of pertinent French/English phrases while we still had Crystal's undivided attention. Then we headed off to finalise arrangements and change some traveller's cheques for Algerian dinars.

---

[3] Tuareg name for the veil-cum-turban all the menfolk wear.

Of course the bank was not officially open, being a holiday and all, but a chance meeting over breakfast with a man claiming to be a teller had led to a lunch invitation at his home and an offer to legally change our money afterwards. The bank manager, the teller believed, would not mind an interruption on his day off to open the building and unlock the safe. Assisting pathetic, linguistically incompetent tourists was his speciality. Was my personal guardian angel working overtime, or were we about to be fleeced?

In other parts of the world, I would have known exactly what to do. In Tamanrasset, I didn't have a clue. The guy was very sincere; you probably could have seen it in his eyes, had his bifocals not been thicker than Coke bottles. He was lonely—that was obvious. He was the only one to have initiated a conversation with us since we'd arrived in the country, and my gut feeling told me he'd be really sad if we misconstrued his generosity for a con. Chris—the cautious one—had us robbed, dead and buried before three that afternoon, but my instincts proved his wrong. We had a nice lunch with the teller, watched a bit of TV together, then cashed in some TCs at the bank. We even got a receipt.

That evening, back at the stinking Tinhinane (there was only enough water for patrons to swill away their excrement and piss once a day) we met an older couple from Switzerland. Their journey of a lifetime had come to an abrupt end three days previously on the Mali/Algerian border. They'd been ambushed at gunpoint, robbed of everything except the clothes they were wearing and left for dead in the middle of nowhere. The people of Tam were looking after them now, as they waited for some money from their embassy and, hopefully, a couple of tickets home. It was a tragic and very sobering story. A lesson in travelling law. It could have happened to anyone ... it could well happen to us.

We got a ride out to Intakarnet's village the next morning, a tiny compound of mud brick homes on the edge of the vast desertscape. Intakarnet's wife and sister helped him load the camels, as we had quickly shown ourselves to be inept in that department, too. Chris kept himself busy filming the whole ritualised procedure and I just generally kept out of the way. One of those old Ships of the Desert was giving me a dirty look, and the last thing I wanted to be wearing on my face was a mask of putrid dromedary phlegm.

I wondered what they made of us—not the camels, the people: Intakarnet, his family and the few neighbours who had wandered over for a gawp. What did they think of our perplexing lives? How could they even contemplate, let alone understand, the complexity of the world we'd so recently left behind? A world where even the most advanced technology was instantly taken for granted? Where a breakthrough one day was a foregone conclusion the next? What would they think of fax machines? Computers? Bundy machines? Mortgages? Drug crimes? Deadlines?

If only we had the words to ask, the time to explain ... Day after day we perform the most difficult, problematic tasks; we subject ourselves to stress and uncertainty; we right the wrongs of God himself, and here we are, about to take a short walk in the desert and we can't even load up a frigging camel.

I did not, on the whole, shun life in the West, but a small part of me would always envy the simplicity of a nomad's life; the lack of clutter, the autonomy. No matter what the sociologists and politicians of the world said in deference to progress, no matter how much I enjoyed the time-saving gismos and relative comfort of urban life, there would always be tides in my life ebbing me towards the other. There would always be days when I believed the grass greener on the other side—even in the face of a drought. The hidden cost of civilisation was freedom and I considered it a privilege—not a right—to be able to trade those two commodities from time to time.

There was no ceremony to mark our departure. Intakarnet and I just turned, waved and started walking. Chris lingered behind to capture our leaving on film, then ran to catch us up.

Prior to leaving Australia, a company called Beyond Productions had approached us re the possibility of filming a documentary series on our African adventures. They had given Chris a Hi-8 video to shoot a sort of pilot or teaser, which they then envisaged presenting at various documentary markets around the world. On securing the obligatory quota of national and international presales, they would send a full-on film crew to join us in the Never-Never, but for the time being the task was Chris's responsibility entirely.

Intakarnet's camels marched to their master's music, and we quickly realised his score had no rests. Camels, apparently, hated standing for any length of time with a load on, so once a journey was under way, there was no stopping it. We would not be able to wait for Chris to set up or break down his equipment; he was destined to spend half his days in the desert on the run.

Tamanrasset's skyline soon disappeared. The silence of the desert engulfed me. The emptiness I'd felt while flying over the Sahara returned threefold, bringing tears to my eyes. I pretended it was sand, driven by the wind.

For all my intention, it was difficult to yield to this desert. Its immediate effect on my spirit was devastating. It was like walking into an artist's impression of the End of the World, a revelation of earth after the Holocaust.

It took me several days to settle into the momentum of the journey. I was still on overdrive, bounding along as if I were late for an important meeting in the city. The four-hour breaks at midday took boredom to new depths—the forced four-hour marches in the mornings and evenings set new heights for resilience. Chris was constantly running ahead and lagging behind for the sake of the damn showreel and I actually begrudged him the effort! At least he had something to do beyond contemplating desolation. At least he could vary the rhythm of his heartbeat.

Mile after mile, hour after hour I moved forward and nothing seemed to change. I approached each swell in the 'ocean without water' with hope in my heart, then drowned in the long-distance view it revealed. More of the bloody same. As far as the eye could see. Mirages were all that defined the horizon.

Eventually the burning gravel seas parted and the second, more significant grouping of the Ahaggar Mountains rose like a spectre from the flames. They were verily awesome formations. Totally fantastic. Like something Salvador Dali might have conceived under the influence of hallucinogens.

Before sacrificing our souls to this, 'The Garden of Hell',[4] we spent some time exploring the settlements and oases scattered in its vicinity. They were hidden from the general view, swallowed by the sheer magnitude of the great Sahara. As inconceivable as it seems, there *was* water out here. People *did* actually live here. They cultivated small pockets of land and irrigated them with water drawn from soaks dug in the sand. They prevailed in small family groups, dwelling in either leather or camel-hair tents, shelters made out of reeds collected from gueltas,[5] or more permanent homes built with mud bricks or concrete.

They kept goats as well as camels—the former providing them with milk, cheese and meat. The task of finding the herd fodder each day fell—as it invariably did in the Third World—to the children. The women tended the fields and it goes without saying really that the men sat around drinking tea all day, speculating on the state of their universe. We were a distraction from the norm and even though theirs was an indifferent welcome, we often found ourselves joining their ceremonious carousals.

Intakarnet was a friend of everyone; he brought news from the city. When he greeted people, the formality of the exchange was quite intriguing. In monotone voices they rattled off a series of formulated questions and responses, asking after each other's God, family, health, wealth and happiness, no doubt. It was like listening to verbal ping-pong. The game usually lasted around five

[4] The local Tuareg name for this region of the Ahaggar.
[5] Pools created by underground springs and streams.

minutes before a change in tone marked the onset of normal conversation.

In many ways this was Intakarnet's journey we were on, not our own, for we stopped when and where he chose to, we met only who he decided we should meet and we passed up the most beautiful camping sites in favour of some highly questionable personal Utopia. Forget 'Midnight at the Oasis'—we were destined to spend our evenings clinging to slag heaps in landscapes not unlike abandoned open quarries. At times Intakarnet left us tending the camels for a few hours while he just wandered off to see a mate without us. We were his vassals—and paying for the honour!

I really don't mean to sound ungrateful; there was just such a distance between the Tuaregs and us. I longed to get closer to them, to learn more from them, but even when we were directly in their presence they remained aloof. The language barrier was a problem and the whole Muslim thing was too—the only contact we had with the women at all was when they came, heads bowed with the indignity of it all, to sell us some pathetic souvenir or present us with a pustular wound they reckoned we could cure. It nearly broke my heart.

Perhaps the Tuaregs were sick to death of tourists, although they hardly found their way out here *en masse*. Maybe the harshness of the desert had scarred more than their skins. Possibly they were preoccupied with thoughts of insurmountable hardship if the present drought refused to break. Whatever the reason, we were not to be permitted to share in anything beyond the occasional cup of nauseating sweet tea, no matter how hard we tried to befriend them. Perhaps we'd have more luck a second time around.

Of the gueltas we were able to explore, the finest lay near Ilaman. Set at the end of a gradually tapering, bone-dry river bed, it was concealed and protected from the elements by a stunning, sheer-sided gorge. Date palms and flowering oleander bushes, vivid green grasses and the appearance of water—albeit just a trickle—lightened our mood immeasurably. Mud underfoot never felt so good!

It was hard to imagine anything, or anyone—other than sculptor Henry Moore—responsible for the shapes and curves of the lower, narrow sections of the gully. It was surely not the work of water—that was too incredible a possibility. But then according to the rock-art found in neighbouring areas, the Ahaggar was once a tropical paradise, running with rivers and teeming with big game of the buffalo, elephant, giraffe and hippo ilk.

Trekking back along the river bed was reminiscent of many a day spent in Pakistan. It was so hot, the heat of the day trapped in a vertical grill made of rock. The water in the guelta had not been fit to drink and we'd run out of the filtered stuff we carried in our bottles. The last five kilometres were an absolute torture, plagued with visions, real and imagined, of dead donkeys and circling vultures.

With relief we reached Ilaman and threw ourselves down to the ground, digging deep with our hands until water seeped to the surface. Intakarnet insisted that the camels drink first.

Before heading off into the wilderness once more, we prepared all the containers we were carrying for water. From here on in, it would be—at best—scarce. Apart from a plastic jerry can, one ten- and two two-litre Cordura water bags, we also had two disembowelled goats to fill. The latter were a Tuareg version of the Spanish wineskin and held about 40 litres each. In theory, water seeped slowly through the pores in the skin and thus kept the hair on the dead goat wet. This, in turn, kept the water inside the 'bag' cool, and consequently sapid. In practice, nothing could have been further from the truth. The grotesque containers leaked like sieves and any water taken from them was anything but palatable. It tasted like a zoo would smell, six months into a keeper's strike. It was so vile I could barely stop myself from heaving at the mere thought of having to drink from it. I swear I could smell its vapour on my breath for weeks.

The next two days in the desert were fierce. The sun branded us with its sheer intensity; the wind turned our skin to leather. The temperature never went below 30°C. My body was so charged with static electricity the hair on my head stood on end and crackled when I tried to brush it. At night, in the dark, I could run my fingers over the nylon mesh screen of our tent and actually see sparks shooting from their tips, as if they were a fistful of welding torches in action. It gave me a slight shock, but it was worth putting up with the pain just to see Chris's reaction to the spectacle. It convinced him, once and for all, that he had indeed married an alien. It was a pity we didn't have a spare light globe floating around in our kit; I probably could have given Uncle Fester a run for his money as well.

The terrain was utterly surreal. We dragged the camels back and forth through a veritable playground of formations, past a stash of massive marbles, in and out of dominoes lined up ready for a fall. Every single ball and block seemed to defy gravity. We imagined ourselves to be inside the toy chest of a giant. Ilaman, the 2729-metre peak from which the nearby village had taken its name, popped up from the centre with the startling, attention-stealing bravado of a jack-in-the-box. For all the world, however, it looked just like an erect uncircumcised penis.

Tucked behind Ilaman, out of sight until we were almost upon it, was Tahat, 'The Beautiful' mountain, the highest peak in the whole Algerian Sahara. Unlike its attendant monoliths, Tahat was not a single tower or weathered dome of rock; it was a rubble pile, a scrap heap left behind once the contract for the building of this desert had expired. While every other climbable feature in the Ahaggar required a certain degree of technical expertise, Tahat's summit was well within the reach of any novice scrambler. By virtue of that fact alone, the mountain was indeed, beautiful.

We camped right at the foot of Tahat, intent on an early start. Leaving Intakarnet and the camels behind, Chris and I managed to climb halfway up the peak before sunrise, thereby making the most of the coolest hours of the day and ensuring we were well positioned by dawn.

Watching day break over the Sahara from this height was just amazing. The huge volcanic plugs which had so dominated the scape from ground-level were dwarfed by the perspective, lost again, as they had been from the air, to the greater panorama of the desert. As light gently reached them they seemed to yawn and stretch, slowly assuming their stiff daytime stance. Ilaman shed his shadow as if it were a satin cape slipping with a flourish from the shoulder of an illusionist.

It didn't take long for the world to be drenched in harsh desert glare and our brows to be once again dripping with sweat. We reached the top and took a good look around. I could have sworn we were on the moon now, looking over its barren, tortured surface from the steep-sided rim of a crater.

We were off Tahat and back at camp by midday. It appeared as if Intakarnet had taken advantage of our absence to do a bit of housekeeping. His entire wardrobe and bedding had been spread out for an airing and his turban lay unravelled at his feet. He was fast asleep beneath a lean-to made from two stunted acacia boughs and a saddle cloth. He was using a rock for a pillow.

I couldn't stop staring at his head. It seemed so small without that great astronaut's helmet of cloth! A grey stubble covered his crown and his face and neck were dyed a deep blue tougoulmust hue. He had tiny little ears and a token nose to match his beadlike eyes. He reminded me of an otter. It was the first time I'd seen any Tuareg man without his ennobling headgear, an unthinkable social gaffe in the presence of foreigners and in-laws! I suspected it was akin to a politician being caught with his pants down. Chris mused that the overall effect was like seeing Darth-Vader remove his mask in the closing scenes of *Star Wars*. To save Intakarnet embarrassment, we tiptoed out of range before making noises that would wake him.

Just after lunch three men appeared with a caravan of 15 snowy camels. They were heading into Tamanrasset to sell off the younger members of their herd. They sat cross-legged on their magnificent mounts; one held a set of reigns between the big and second toes of his right foot and the others had them twisted around their saddle pommels and fingers. Each wore a pure white *tougoulmust*.

You could tell by the way they carried themselves and sat so straight-backed and head-high in their mobile thrones, that they were keenly aware of the impression they were creating—an unassailably regal, fearfully masculine image I would hold in my mind's eye forever. It was everything the desert was meant to be, according to the celluloid promise. Any minute now, one of those dashing Tuaregs would swoop down, scoop me up and whisk me away across the dunes to his hideaway harem in the hills ...

The next morning we woke to a peculiar tapping on the roof of our tent. It was not Raoul, the incessant Drummer of Death; it was Rain! The Giver of Life! After five years the drought had broken!

Chris was screaming, '*Shitta*! *Shitta*!'[6] and Intakarnet was giggling his head off like a little boy. Every day Chris had teased our guide with knowing glances at the sky and a vow that it would rain before our time in the desert was up. Here we were—not on our final day in the Sahara, but certainly on the last we would spend with Intakarnet—and the Heavens were ensuring he would remember it forever!

Well, for 35 seconds anyway. It was the shortest droughtbreaker in living memory. Not enough to lay the dust but sufficient to win Chris the bet I'd made with him the previous evening

---

[6] That Arabic word he knew to mean 'rain'.

when his supposed 'rain leg' had indicated a drop in barometric pressure.

Clouds continued to roam the sky for the remainder of the morning, which kept the temperature down to a very pleasant 20°C. By the time we reached Assekrem, the site of Father Charles de Foucauld's famous reclusive hermitage, it had dropped to 10° and we couldn't break out the pile jackets and beanies fast enough.

Intakarnet left with his camels at around 1pm, and Chris and I settled into a room inside a refuge built expressly for tourists (and pilgrims with a higher purpose) just below the chapel and cells comprising the Retreat.

The latter was built in 1905 by Père de Foucauld, a one-time inheritably wealthy, over-indulgent womaniser-turned-soldier-turned-explorer-turned-spy-turned-Trappist Monk-turned-hermit. He had chosen the site for its incomparable solitude, believing that its elevation and splendour put him as close to God as he could get on earth. Revered by the local inhabitants, he lived up there in seclusion and poverty, compiling a Tuareg dictionary, until 1916, when he was murdered by fanatic Muslims.

The hermitage still functioned; a small band of monks performed a daily mass at sunrise and a continuous stream of visitors came from all corners of the world to pay homage to Foucauld, God and the view that had helped make the two one.

They started to arrive at around four o'clock, a dusty motorcade led by a party of deeply tanned French couples and their intoxicating scent of expensive perfume. They would have looked more at home on a ski-slope. Next came some German overlanders who quickly drove in, took a few photos and vanished—celebrated sunset unseen. Their objective was not to touch the land—or to be touched by it—but to cover as much distance as they could in the shortest time possible. The motivation for being here was neither spiritual nor physical; it was all just a matter of logistics.

A Danish team on cross-country trail bikes roared in, their leathers covered in a sizeable portion of the grand Sahara. When they took off their helmets and goggles, they looked just like laughing clowns. A Christian youth group from Paris staggered in *sans* camels—they were tethered at the foot of Assekrem where they could forage overnight.

They kept coming: a wave as endless as any other surging through the Sea of Sand. By 5pm there were 200, all crowded together on the sacrosanct lookout on top of Assekrem.

It really was a remarkable view, worthy of—indeed commanding—reverence. Even in this barren, lifeless, earthly void, divinity held court. God and the Devil were one, the majesty co-eternal . . .

The last of the Ahaggar's monumental ghost castles and soaring cathedrals were slowly secreted away for the night, wrapped in Christo-like shrouds of heavy canvas darkness.

Chris and I stayed on, long after the other tourists had left, shivering together alone on the mountain, straining to hear the voice of the desert again. Until its whisper had been so overwhelmed, I had not even known it could speak. Until its aura had been so lain to waste, I had not even known it could feel.

We were leaving the Sahara, but in our hearts we knew the Sahara would never leave us. It had touched us with both its hostility and beauty, awed us with its magnitude and guile, wooed us with its silence.

THE MARRAKESH
EXPRESS

HE DIN WAS deliciously terrifying, enticing. We could hear it from several blocks away, calling like the strains of some wild student demonstration or Chinese New Year parade. It took great restraint on my part to stay by Chris's side as he completed the hotel check-in formalities: I was hungry to the point of madness for a piece of the action downtown, impatient for the sensory assault in store.

I had read so many descriptions of Marrakesh, seen so many photographs of its medieval souks and side shows, that I couldn't wait to experience all it had to offer first-hand. Every minute spent at the reception desk of some ho-hum flophouse was literally a minute stolen from my life.

We hit the streets straight after stowing our kit in the room. It was 5pm on the last Sunday in April, and thousands of people

Morocco

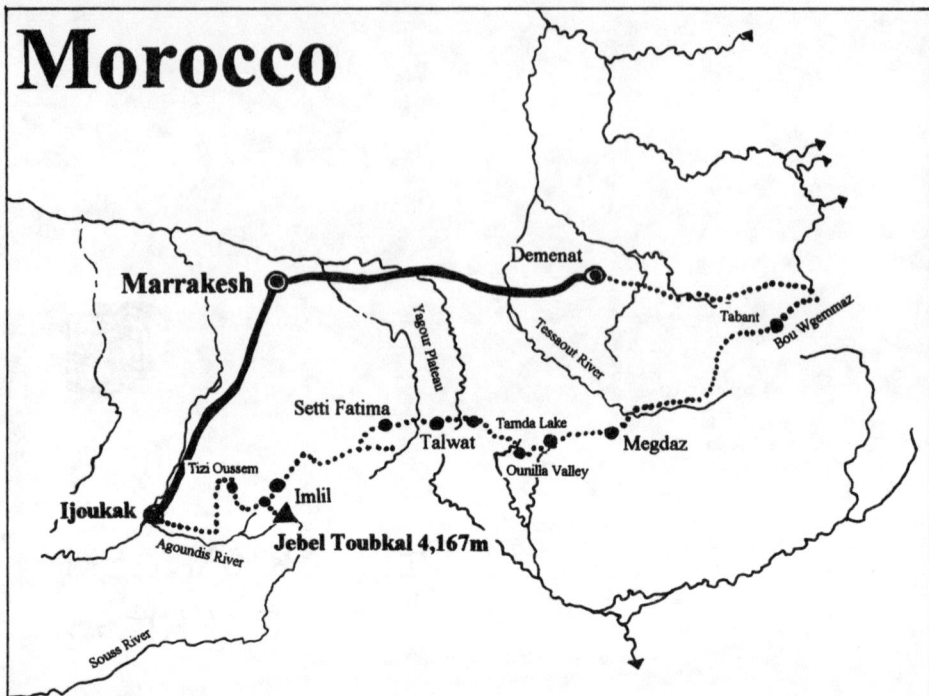

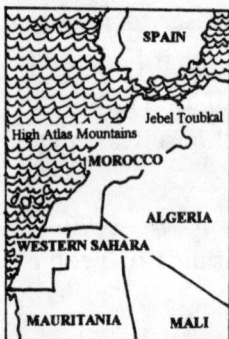

were buzzing through the narrow alleys of the Medina[1] towards Djemma el Fna, 'The Assembly Place of the Nobodies'. They swarmed into the plaza like so many worker bees foraging for nectar.

As soon as Chris and I neared the famous square, we were besieged by a dozen 'unofficial guides'. Their job was not to actually lead or enlighten; for 20 dirhams[2] an hour they would simply ward off others of their kith.

Overtures like 'No thank you,' 'Please leave me alone,' 'Get lost' and 'Rack off!' had no effect whatsoever. It was less stressful to just go along with the con, and pay one of them to accompany you into the vortex.

A long time ago this square was marked out with the decapitated heads of insubordinates, lopped and pickled at the behest of the sultan and vaunted in deference to his rule. Today the executioner's spoils have vanished and the perimeter of the vast arena is defined on its two open sides by a less intimidating line of umbrellaed carts, alternately stacked to the hilt with oranges and sugar-coated peanuts. Beyond them, all semblance of order dissolved; one great whirlwind of enterprise and entertainment ensued.

Anybody who was Nobody was there. Could-have-been magicians, would-be storytellers and has-been musicians performed to a tight circle of fans. The minstrels rattled iron castanets and banged on camel-skin drums with long hooked canes. The raconteurs delivered their distorted, earpiercing tales through portable public address systems. Collectively they were responsible for at least half the cacophony we'd heard from the hotel.

Soothsayers, beggars, hustlers and thieves worked the bewildered crowd. Teenage mutant acrobats cartwheeled between them, hunchback snake-charmers slithered amidst them, lunatics and self-mutilators wandered among them; the whole gamut of

---

[1] A North African word meaning the original city precinct, or native quarter of the city.
[2] The local currency—at that time the exchange rate was approximately five dirhams to the Australian dollar.

nether-world luminaries were there, as if they'd just arisen from a painting by Brueghel or Bosch.

Costumed water-vendors roamed around, drawing attention to themselves by ringing bells. It was no longer customary to buy a drink from them—they preferred it if you just took their photo. At 10 dirhams per frame the fall from tradition to tourism was hardly surprising. They really looked a picture, though, in their tasselled sombreros and heavy leather aprons covered in brass coins and highly polished cups.

The dentists were equally photogenic, displaying their innumerable human extractions on rickety folding tables and tarps. I thought the rusty pliers they each evidenced were a particularly nice touch.

Herbalists hawked the questionable benefits of their dried chameleon and desiccated lizard elixirs by contorting their bodies into totally inhuman positions. Prophets decried the moot advantages of their faith by surrounding themselves with half-witted converts. Witch doctors did themselves even greater disservice by appearing to be irretrievably dead.

Everywhere I turned an image formed, one bizarre vision after the other, portending a delirium of absurd revelations. Colours, smells and sounds collided, like fragments inside a multisensory kaleidoscope. I was lost in an eternity of aberration and horror.

After what seemed like hours we made our way over to the food stalls, and a hundred different aromas rushed to tease another sense. The smell of kerosene, burning in lamps now that darkness was nigh, was overpowered by scents strictly gourmet in nature. Hot oil sizzled in oversized woks, meat singed on charcoal grills, snails simmered in their shells in mammoth vats of brine, entrails waited to be added to soups. The air was redolent with dubious temptation.

At some point, the end of the 30-ring circus of Djemma el Fna became the beginning of the thousand-and-one emporiums which made up the heart of the city's Medina. This was as close as we would ever get to a living history and with each step forward we were verily transported back in time.

It was like a scene from Ali Baba and the Forty Thieves. A maze of arteries led us into chambers dripping with silver and gold, past atriums chock-a-block with carpets, into ventricles stuffed with leatherwork and wool. Each passageway in the labyrinthine organ was a vein, pumping and throbbing with the energy of a particular trade. A gentle murmur hummed through the alley where people Singered clothes, a clangorous racket resounded down the street of the ironworkers, a metrical tapping could be heard in the grimy backblocks of the coppersmiths. There were dyers' markets reeking of lanolin and steam, spice markets pungent with their potpourri fare, woodturners fashioning furniture on foot-operated lathes, hide-tanners flogging their freshly killed wares, and at least a kilometre's length of merchants hawking hand-made leather boots and bags. My favourite stalls were those selling embroidered *babouches*,[3] fanned out like peacock tails on all sides of their box-like cubicles.

Apart from pedestrians, the only traffic permitted on the constricted vessels of the Medina were carts and barrows drawn by donkeys. The alleys were never wide enough for both, and we were constantly throwing ourselves into doorways and displays to save ourselves from harm. The way those asses took the blind corners was enough to give even a veteran bull-runner a coronary!

The Medina was an incredible phenomenon, a magical cornucopia. It would take days, even weeks, to explore the entire entity, but to feel its pulse—even briefly—was to know that you yourself were alive in the world.

With this first encounter momentarily satisfying my hunger for urban adventure, we were free to focus on the mountain-based one we'd actually come to Morocco to have. There would be plenty of opportunities to recconaître the souks later, when we'd

---

[3] Pointed Moroccan slippers.

completed trekking the whole high Atlas, and before and after our scheduled *60 Minutes* interview. According to the latest correspondence from the producer responsible for the story, they were due to join us in Marrakesh in the last week of May.

In the mad months leading up to our departure from Australia, we'd made contact with the Imzilen Brothers, a Moroccan agency specialising in organising ski and çlimbing trips in the High Atlas range. These were normally of five days' length, but our plan for something a bit meatier had not daunted them. They faxed through a well-thought-out four-week itinerary 'prepared with precision', and promised us the pick of their affable guides: one Mohammed 'Kalhal' Bouchahoud, fluent in English and—as 'uncredible *(sic)* as it seems'—ours for the duration of the trek!

It all seemed too easy, too casual to be true after Algeria. One day, having returned to the belligerent capital from the depths of the Sahara, we were ducking for cover every time a car backfired—the next we were in Morocco, revelling in its imperturbable charm. And now we were off to meet the latest in what was quickly shaping up to be a long line of Mohammeds, at the restaurant on the lower floor of our hotel for a late-night snack of pigeon pie and soda!

Kalhal—as everyone but his mother called him—was every bit as wonderful as we had hoped. Built like a string bean, he had a gentle, unusually dark face, an artist's hands, a fabulous smile, a soft voice, eccentric laugh and a wad of uncharacteristically frizzy hair. We sat with him for an hour, getting the low-down on the mountains and coming to grips with the basics of the Berber language—much to the delight of the restaurant's waiters. The Imzilen Brothers couldn't have chosen a more compatible guide if they'd known Chris and me as intimately as we knew each other. We couldn't have been more pleased and excited if Kalhal had arrived gift-wrapped!

We left Marrakesh at ten the next morning, bound for the High

Atlas village of Ijoukak. The Imzilen Brothers had arranged for our mulers to meet us there, but I couldn't believe such a complicated plan, arranged without the aid of telephones, would work. It certainly wouldn't in any other part of the world, so why should it in Morocco?

After an hour speeding across the flat, red Haouz Plains which surrounded the cypress and palm-flecked oasis of Marrakesh, we hit the foothills of the High Atlas Mountains. Cloud obscured the tops of all but the least significant peaks, yet the valleys between them were clear for the viewing. They were simply beautiful, patchworked with almond trees and handkerchief fields of tender young wheat. The tiny hamlets within the landscape emerged from the purple-red soil as picture-perfect as if they were conjured from a fairytale.

The vision was made all the more fantastic by our recent depravation. The lasting impression we carried from the desert was completely devoid of the colour green—to see it now, in such vivid abundance, was to truly see it for the first time.

All my doubts about our logistical arrangements proved groundless when we finally reached Ijoukak. All that anxiety for nothing! There were our mulers, standing by the roadside, as nonchalant as school kids waiting for a bus. It was just too good to be true! Aside from the gods, the sun was even momentarily shining down on us!

Kalhal introduced us to the diminutive 50-something Bouchma and his nuggetty 37-year-old nephew, Lahcen. We shook hands, loaded up their charges and, without any ado at all, headed straight for the hills. Poor Chris didn't even have time to set up the video.

For the first hour we walked as if in a dream; an arbour of olive trees dappling the light across the cobblestoned trail underfoot. A light breeze rustled the new green leaves of an ancient walnut grove; sunshine spilt from the lips of a canyon and dribbled down its rust-blushed chin. The river, swollen with melted snow from as-yet-unseen peaks, sang clean and pure below, and laughter peeled from darkened doorways as we passed by. Warm smiles and giggles met our heavily accented attempts to say 'G'day' in Tachelhit, the dialect spoken by the Cheleuh tribes of the Berbers. The whole scene was extraordinarily idyllic. I had to keep pinching myself to prove it was real.

A predominantly fair-skinned race, the Berbers were a people with mysterious origins. Because they had lived in northwestern Africa since before the time of the Pharaohs, many anthropologists linked them with the Egyptians and Libyans. Others maintained they were related to Southern Europeans of Iberian stock. No one knew for certain, but in any event, they were Morocco's first known inhabitants.

Their name, some authorities believed, was derived from the notion that they were the 'original Barbarians'. Historically they have been described as a brave and formidable people, and by one source as 'the greatest thieves, traitors and assassins in the world.'[4] Even the French, who ruled most of Morocco from 1912, took 21 bloody years to subdue these mountain tribes, only to hand back the baton of Independence in 1956.

Goliath was said to be a Berber. Bouchma and Lahcen, our mulers, were as well—only they were about as menacing and hostile as teddy bears. Their true colours were reflected in the pastel hues of their *jellabas*,[5] and together with Kalhal they were surely paving the way for a new social identity. These three wise men were the nucleus of a new breed: Morocco's foremost Sensitive New Age Guys.

Our first day on the High Atlas trail ended at Taghaghist, a small village clinging precariously to the side of a cliff, several hundred metres above the Agoundis River. It was not a place I would have chosen to raise even the most genetically sure-footed children, but obviously the Berbers in these parts had nothing to

---

[4] A comment by the great Christian historian, Africanus.
[5] The long, full-sleeved, loose, hooded garment worn throughout Morocco.

fear. Somewhere along the line, velcro had been engineered into the DNA of their prodigy's soles.

The wind had picked up, bearing a chill in it direct from the summits we hoped to climb. It looked like rain was on its way. We had intended camping, but the ominous not-too-distant clouds—not to mention the distinct lack of horizontal space—shot our plan to pieces. Accepting a gracious offer of semi-commercial hospitality, we bedded down on prayer rugs in the spartan yet warm home of Ait Ben Ochen.[6]

Ait Ben Ochen, and many other Berbers like him, regularly shared his domicile with infidels. It brought in a little extra cash, and that was useful in these trying economic times. Few foreigners passed this way, but our host knew how to ask all the right questions ('You want my house?' 'You want eat food?') in English, French, Arabic, Italian and even Spanish.

Ait Ben Ochen treated us to our first Moroccan mint tea ceremony, and early the next morning shared a huge communal bowl of milky rice porridge and butter. According to our Three Musketeers, we were in for a pretty steep climb and, after yesterday's effort, they figured we could use all the help we could get. This special breakfast—the first of four square meals the hearty Berbers usually consumed in a day—would get us to the top of the first pass, no worries.

We had our own selection of dried fruit and nuts to assist us on the descent of that particularly steep ridgeline, and the gorgeous views along the way carried us through to Asoul. It was breathtaking country, this High Atlas and it sure took the weight of the world from my shoulders!

I couldn't get over how small the cultivated terraces and plots were in these mountains. In some cases, it hardly seemed as if it were worth the effort. And yet irrigation canals fed the lot of them, drawing water from distant springs and streams. Wherever

---

[6] *Ait* or *Ayt* means 'son/s of'.

there was soil there was a verdant patch, sown with wheat or grasses for the cattle and ringed with purple irises. The latter, Kalhal adamantly insisted, were grown for medicinal uses, and not some higher SNAG purpose. He nearly rolled off the mountainside when I attempted to suggest as much.

The terrain, if anything, was steeper than my beloved Himalaya. Either that, or I was hopelessly out of condition. But even the tonka-tough victim had to admit he was feeling the gradient in his thighs and calves.

By the time we reached the summer pastures above Tizi Oussem the following evening we were ready to throw in the towel. Aching all over, the thought of crossing the Tazâghart Pass with full packs was not only unpleasant, it seemed damned impossible. The route we had unwittingly chosen to reach Jebel Toubkal[7] was not negotiable by mule, so Bouchma, having earlier agreed to take our trusty pack-bearers back to his own village of Imlil via a lower, circuitous route, asked us to give him all the equipment and food we would not be requiring for our separate journey. Once we'd crossed the pass and climbed the mountain, we would head down the valley, reunite with Bouchma and the mules and continue our High Atlas trek. Lahcen would help us carry our climbing gear over to Toubkal, but shunned the opportunity to climb the peak with us. He'd only done it about a hundred times and reckoned he was too old now to bother.

Bouchma had every intention of staying the night with us before retracing his steps to Tizi Oussem; the mules, however, did not. Just on dusk, they took off at great speed, as if they'd been spooked by a ghost. Poor old Bouchma went flying after them, but he didn't catch the runaways until they reached the village itself, about an hour and a half down the valley. They finally struggled back into camp shortly after 9pm.

Bouchma was laughing and skylarking about, having seen a

[7] Jebel is the Arabic word for Mountain. At 4167m Toubkal is the highest peak in North Africa.

funny side to the whole episode. For the remainder of our trek through Morocco he would refer to the incident every time he thought someone needed a bit of a lift. We would tease him about it constantly, calling out 'Tizi Oussem' every morning when we woke to find the hobbled mules had ventured out of sight in search of fodder.

The next morning we were up at the crack of dawn, packing and preparing for the split. Bouchma hugged us all and sang his way off into the distance. We implored the will of Allah, hoisted on our backpacks and headed slowly uphill.

The Azzaden valley grew steadily narrower. The morning grew steadily colder. The stream we seemed to cross continuously slowed to an icy trickle.

After several hours the valley became a gorge and the gorge became a chasm. We were not climbing this massif—we were entering it via some secret passage. We were inside a veritable cathedral of stone, clawing our way over verglas[8] boulders and inching along gargoyled cornices and overhanging ledges. Massive waterfalls, yet to thaw from their wintering, hung like chandeliers overhead. Smaller, flowing ones filled the whole nave with their thunder. The lofty ramparts of the Tazâghart ridgeline loomed higher still.

We stopped briefly at Lépiney Hut, a little-used refuge for climbers halfway up the Azzaden. What lay beyond it was utterly fearsome and we started to think we'd bitten off a little more than we could chew. We were trekkers by trade, but this little epic looked way out of our league. To take on something this tough so early on in the expedition was madness.

We climbed—on all fours—up a wall of sliding scree. As if to insult our ineptitude, the gods began spitting in disgust. We hadn't noticed the weather closing in; there had just been too many other things to keep our eye on. It was too late to turn back now. Wind and mist enveloped the view.

[8] A thin layer of clear ice covering the surface of the rock.

Kalhal encouraged us. Lahcen fell silent. We reached the top of the ridge and collapsed into separate gaps in its saw-tooth edge. Another, higher one lay ahead, on the opposite side of a steep snowfield, glistening with firnspiegel.[9] I remembered that our rope was on its way to Imlil . . .

I looked at Chris. He looked at me. Our fear was palpable. It did not need to find words. Our faces said it all.

We'd run out of water and the scant food we were carrying was failing to give us the boost we so desperately required. My throat was so dry it took all the energy I had just to swallow the lump of dried-out Berber damper I'd been attempting to chew. It was freezing cold and as if to express how I felt about getting across the treacherous mirrored snowslope ahead, I started to shiver uncontrollably.

I was losing body heat fast. We had to make a move before I became hypothermic. I had never felt so afraid of losing control.

We strapped on our crampons. I felt better once we hit the snow and started working our way across it. Chris felt considerably worse. It was the first time he had ever attempted to use the spiked steel boot attachments, and no amount of reassurance would bolster his confidence. To further aid his grip on the surface, Lahcen, Kalhal and I took turns at cutting deep steps through to the snow with our ice axes.

I will never forget the intense look of concentration and unadulterated terror etched across Chris's face as he made his way slowly over the slope. Or the consuming guilt I felt for having led this shy, sensitive ABC cameraman so far out of his comfort zone. When he made it across, he was as clammy as a sponge. He confided he had not been able to look down the sweep of the icy face for fear of turning to jelly and falling. If he had, it would surely have been the end of him.

We hugged briefly, then clamoured over rocks and patchy snow

---

[9] A thin layer of ice formed on snow.

to the top of the second jagged ridgeline of Tazâghart Pass.

We couldn't see too far afield, given the swirling sombre mist, and all hope of seeing Jebel Toubkal faded faster than the light. Kalhal was disappointed for us, but we were so relieved to have reached the end of the climb, we really didn't give a damn about the lack of view. Being alive was reward enough for our efforts.

It was getting late in the day and descending before nightfall was not just a priority—it had become a matter of life and death. To lose our way in this terrain, or to be benighted in such a clime, would be utterly fatal.

The way down was innocent of trail, and we were extremely glad to have someone with Kalhal's experience guiding us. There was no way we could have figured out a route on our own, even without the hindering fog.

We threw ourselves off the pass like a couple of lemmings. Landing on our butts, we quickly righted ourselves into glissading positions and 'surfed' the rough leeward scree. We plunge-stepped down one sheer couloir,[10] zigzagged hand over heel for several kilometres on loose rock and panicked when several times the thickening pea-souper made it impossible to see what lay beyond our own noses, let alone the next bend. It got so bad we had to hold on to each other as blind people might in unfamiliar territory, too wary to move.

At one point we had to put all our faith in Kalhal's ability to judge exactly where we were on the hypothetical map with nothing but his sixth sense for a compass. How I wished we'd invested 10 dirham in some hejab amulet from the Medina ...

Trying not to focus for too long on the possible dire consequences, we flung ourselves into space, hoping and praying we'd land quickly on some preferably soft surface.

Just on nightfall we reached Neltner Hut, another but much

[10] A gully; usually with a base of snow or ice. It often provides the easiest route through steep rock.

larger lodge for climbers at the foot of Jebel Toubkal. We could barely believe we'd made it!

Kalhal prised open the heavy door and a great rush of warm air hit us like a wall of heat escaping from a blast furnace. At least 50 pairs of incredulous eyes met our own. I doubt I could have been more surprised if it were my birthday and the crowd were all friends!

Everyone was yelling—in at least ten languages—for us to shut the door. You didn't need to be a polyglot to understand what they wanted; you could just tell. The overpowering aroma of Channel No 5 and *Une Homme* unmasked the nationality of at least half the temporary occupants of the hut. The rest, wearing an assortment of European designer-label headbands and padded jackets, were predominantly blond. There was an atmosphere of *après* ski; a certain *je ne sais quoi*/social-page buzz in the air. And regrettably, we appeared to be the only ones having a bad hair day.

Recognising Kalhal and Lahcen, a few of the local guides and tour group rouseabouts wriggled along on the cushioned bench they had commandeered just behind the door, and made room for the four of us. On learning where we'd been they at least showed how impressed they were, by chiding Kalhal for even attempting the route so early in the season.

The caretaker of the hut pressed a hot cup of mint tea into my hands. I settled back on the bench with Chris and Kalhal and together we toasted the day. I didn't think I had ever been so tired or so content. My aching body just seemed to melt into the furniture and my mind dissolved in the atmosphere. I closed my eyes and went out like a light. The ecstasy of surrender was never so sweet.

The majority of the tour-group summiteers were up at 3 o'clock next morning. Stove jets were fired up, ski stocks were readied, additional perfume was applied, coffee was brewed and the table was spread with a breakfast of crusty bread sticks and apricot jam. It was part of the regime here, as it was on the really big mountains of the Himalaya, to start climbing well before dawn. You then had the best possible chance to get to the top and back before nightfall, or in this case, to see the sunrise from the summit and make it back to Marrakesh that evening for the direct flight to gay Paris.

We had no intention whatsoever of getting up that early and defiantly waited until the last of the jet set had left before inching ourselves from the warmth and security of our sleeping cocoons.

At 5.30am I looked outside and up at the mountain. A continuous line of torches zigzagged across the lower reach of the west face, making it look as benign as a Christmas tree strung with fairylights.

Being an Australian, born and raised in a land as open as it is free, I found the Freudian way Europeans walked *en masse* in the wilderness completely confounding—as if the need to queue was an instinct which did not pay heed to situation or surroundings. Day or night, in foul weather or fair, they marched heel-to-toe like soldier ants, oblivious to—or perhaps intimidated by—the endless space encircling them. Toubkal was no exception; if anything it had encouraged them to squash even closer together. The space between each person was narrower than that between a poster and the wall.

We waited until the first light of dawn before venturing off from the hut. It was absolutely freezing trekking in the shadow of the Toubkal massif and no amount of exertion would warm the old extremities. By the time we reached the summit ridgeline and fell into the path of the morning sun, it was so windy the effect of the direct rays was completely counteracted. We were seriously underdressed for the occasion and suffering for our misjudgment. At least I could keep my hands pretty well confined to my pockets; poor Chris had to keep his thinly gloved fingers free to operate the video camera.

There were some exciting moments on the way to the top, but

nothing to rival the previous day's crossing of Tazâghart Pass—
except, of course, the incongruous view. It was as clear as crystal
up there on the roof of North Africa, standing in snow, shivering
to death, staring out at the vast, desolate, stinking hot Sahara little
more than a stone's throw to the south.

We were totally exhausted by the time we returned to Neltner
Hut and barely able to contemplate, let alone endure, the trek to
Imlil. We couldn't stay at Toubkal because the next army of reg-
imented tourists were already arriving and every single scrap of
space had been reserved. Some patrons, the caretaker confided,
would be sleeping on and under the tables.

With the summit 'bagged', the only thing propelling us forward
was the promise of a hot shower at the hotel four hours further
down the valley. It was a crippling walk for no other reason save
our sad and sorry state, but we arrived in fairly good time.
Bouchma was there to meet us, shaking his happy little head in
disbelief: we really looked like we'd been dragged to hell and back
and no end of steaming water would rid our bodies of fatigue.
We needed a serious vacation in the Bahamas, but Allah had other
plans. We were back on the high trail at 11 o'clock the next
morning.

A week passed before we gave ourselves the luxury of a full
day off. It was a fabulous week though, and the change in scenery
and pace as we trekked from Imlil to the Ounilla Valley was as
good as a holiday, anyway. We walked from village to village, in
and out of magnificent valleys, over several snow-covered passes,
between green and yellow pastures, across carpets of wildflowers
fresh with morning dew. More than once I imagined myself to be
back at home in the Himalaya.

Walnut trees waited for the onset of summer, their wiry old
skeletons draped in cobwebs of mist. Cloud rollicked in from the
west, plastering the last of the season's snow on the parapets of
the fortressed mountains. Streams ran like mercury between silent
ravines, rivers ran like music through tranquil glens and dales.

Range after rugged range, pass after gruelling pass, valley after verdant valley—the beauty of it all washed over us and cleansed our spirits anew.

We spent the nights camping near *azibs*[11] or sleeping in simple rooms as guests of a particular new friend or distant relative of Kalhal's. Each and every village was a gem caught in the rough claw of a mountainside, a pearl on a pylon encrusted with shell. Taking their hue from the rock and soil of the landscape, they rose in celebration of its variance. Some villages were blood-red, others greyish green and white.

The narrow streets and alleys between the adobe dwellings were so medieval I was sure we had fallen into a world beyond time. Old men rode by, side-saddle on their stocky mounts, concealed in long hooded robes; children whooshed small flocks of sheep from their overnight pens; women lugged grasses from the fields to make haystacks; chickens scratched in the dirt for a long-forgotten or overlooked grain. The forlorn magpie cry of the muezzin, calling a community to prayer from the minaret of a humble village mosque, echoed through the Dantesque landscape five times a day and the only even vaguely automated sound on the breeze was that of a shuttle, picking through the warp threads of an antique family loom.

We moved from the Moorish Middle Ages right back to a time predating all recorded history. On the windswept high plateau of Yagour we ran our fingers over drawings etched into slabs of stone five or 10 thousand years ago, petroglyphs of the sun, of knives and battle scenes, of horses and shields. Right in the centre of the open-air museum, bringing us back to the present with a start, was a shepherd boy's laboured impression of a helicopter.

From the plateau we trekked down into a valley filled with honey-pot hills which flowed into a gorge filled with flowering oleanders. Young girls ran from the fields of connecting vales with

[11] Shepherds' huts, made of stone, usually situated in the summer pasture areas high in the mountains.

posies of scarlet poppies and kisses for my weathered hands. They
wanted nothing, just to touch and smile. Their beauty went so
much deeper than the doeskin of their cheeks. Their brothers
came to our camp in the evening and, after a lengthy discussion
among themselves, put on a little impromptu display of acrobatic
feats.

By the time we reached Afra the landscape had changed again.
It was bare, arid, worn out—lying in the lap of time like two
ancient gnarled hands clasped in quiet contemplation. Each
arthritic knuckle was one ridge closer to the dead heart of the
Sahara.

We skirted this other-worldly land and crossed into the resplendent valley of Telouet. It was so wide and green, so flat and fertile,
and in the centre of it all there lay a fabulous *kasbah*.

The 19th century ancestral castle, strategically situated on the
Timbuktu to Fez caravan route, was once a stronghold for the
Glaoui Berbers, the feudal lords of the High Atlas. From this
shadowy labyrinth they were able to monitor the movement of
gold, salt and slave caravans across the Sahara and keep the
farmers in the fertile oasis regions under tight control. The *kasbah's* exterior was fast crumbling away but inside, one of the
musty reception rooms had been preserved for posterity.

Kalhal tracked down the keymaster, a portly dude in military
greens and a beret. We paid him the obligatory entrance fee, took
possession of a huge silver key, and followed our guide down a
formally whitewashed, empty corridor. The key unlocked two
intricately painted and carved doors inlaid with silver damascene
which paled the instant they were opened. The rooms behind were
simply astonishing.

Floor to soaring domed ceiling, the walls and elaborate
archways were covered in multi-coloured faïence mosaics and
intricately patterned plaster, carved in such a way that it resembled fine lace or honeycomb. Magic numbers and passages from
the Koran were worked into the designs. Every square centimetre

was a work of art unto itself. The craftsmanship was amazing, but the mood of the time capsule was really quite disturbing. The place was definitely haunted—no doubt by the ghosts of those formerly enslaved by the local caids.

The window frames held huge, elaborate wrought-iron grilles. From them, you could look down on the lush green fields of the serfs' descendants, and out to the raw, bleeding, tired old mountains beyond. The contrast was stunning, but it left me cold. It said too much about a system I abhorred, one which was thankfully overthrown at independence.

Over the week our friendship with our guide and charismatic mulers had strengthened, and we were now pretty much part of their extended Berber 'family'. We were coming to grips with the rudiments of Tachelhit and had even learnt a song which we'd sing at the top of our lungs as we wandered through the mountains. Kalhal had shown himself to be quite the philosopher; for him trekking was a metaphor for life: 'Sometimes you go up, sometimes you go down . . . ' Old Bouchma, his crocheted skullcap superglued to his balding head, was adept at turning every photo opportunity into a big hugging session, and Lahcen was constantly giving and receiving cheek. He had a bottomless travelling wardrobe and every day he'd model some new garment he claimed he'd received from a satisfied tourist 'girlfriend'. He was desperate to add an Australian to his own version of a 'Favoured Nations' status list and constantly schemed and begged Chris to bring him a suitable selection of candidates—disguised, of course, as an all-female trekking party. Allah forbid if his wife ever found out!

Bouchma and Lahcen couldn't understand a word of English, but every night I would read them the opening passages from *Out of Africa*. My Meryl Streep impersonation really tickled them and they would roll all over the place in hysterics. Her photo on the back cover had become an icon.

We spent our sacred day off with Kalhal's immediate family in

Tiourza, and visited several relations living in other villages of the Ounilla Valley. Kalhal's brood were not part of your ordinary family tree; their plotted genealogy looked more like a strangler fig than your atypical upside-down oak. Closest to home, Kalhal and his younger brother had married two sisters, who just so happened to be their first cousins. This meant their aunty was also their mother-in-law. Her younger sister's son had married one of Kalhal's three sisters, but we didn't meet them since they lived in France with their five children—who I guess must have been Kalhal's second cousins *and* his nephews and nieces. It grew more complicated than that the further back you ventured.

Chris and the fellas spent much of the day lounging around the house listening to the radio and eating. I joined Kalhal's wife and mum down by the river for a major washing session, then learnt the finer art of *couscous* preparation in the dingy kitchen, separated from the main body of the house by a postage-stamp courtyard-cum-pen. We had really grown fond of the traditional cuisine, especially the steamed, buttery staple, and *tajine* of the day—a stew of mixed vegetables and some kind of meat. It was always served in a huge mound and eaten communally.

After meal number three (the equivilent of lunch taken at afternoon tea time), I wandered off by myself to check out the valley. The way the sun set over it was like nothing I'd ever seen on earth; the exposed soils and dull-by-day mountainsides glowed with the deepest reds, the warmest oranges, the duskiest pinks and the palest apricot hues. They were rough terracotta and smooth porcelain crucibles, piled haphazardly on top of one another, firing in a vast *raku* kiln.

Many of the houses, incandescent in the light on the far side of the Ounilla Valley, were large and new, built by Berbers flaunting the monetary benefits of countless hours spent in the mines of Lyons in France. Most only got to enjoy their comparatively palatial creations for two weeks every few years, though; the rest of the time they were away from their cherished homeland, living in pokey flats, scrimping and saving for the biennial airfares. Doubtlessly the children of the migrant labourers enjoyed a better education abroad, but their monolingual provincial mothers were virtually imprisoned in their apartments by the language barrier and unbridgeable cultural gulf that existed between them and their indigenous neighbours. Seeing their homes and knowing they were empty filled me with sadness. It was true that life for a Moslem woman—no matter how liberal[12]—was by Western standards an incarceration in itself, but at least on their home turf they were walled in by familiarity and security; they had other women to gossip to and an extended family to help them with the daily chores. In Lyons they were alone. The only voices they had to interrupt their day were the unintelligible ones droning away on the radio and TV.

Beyond the Ounilla Valley the mountainsides were literally on fire, not just baking in the sunset glow, but going up in smoke. The last forests cloaking the range between Tiourza and Tamda Lake—site of our camp the following evening—were being felled and pit-fired to produce charcoal. Caravans of sooty donkeys and mules ferried the fuel down to the roadhead at Tiourza and a full lorryload a day departed for some distant market.

Too many of Morocco's mountains were being denuded: the government actually issued licences for such destruction. The army's reafforestation campaign, mounted in 1986 to forestall further denudation of the nation, had amounted to too little too late. A few thousand eucalyptus saplings were all there was to show for the gesture. It was obvious with even a cursory glance over the terrain, let alone a long trek across it, that few people were interested in the future of the environment—just in the revenue it could raise here and now, the food it could cook here and now and the roof it would support here and now. Resources were there to exploit, not protect, and so what if the desert

---

[12] Rural Berbers practised a more relaxed version of the faith—for example, they did not wear the veil, as was customary among the more orthadox Moslim sects.

expanded upwards as well as outwards? It was the Will of Allah. It was also the too-often-repeated story of the tomorrowless Third World.

The smooth hills on either side of the twin lakes of Tamda were totally naked breasts of scree, ravaged by a process as thoughtless and indelible as incestuous rape. The lakes were pooled tears, one sapphire, one turquoise, shed by Mother Nature over her own children's continual abuse.

From Tamda we stumbled along the edge of the High Atlas, pummelled by a wind roaring up from the floor of the great Sahara. It followed us across the arid ranges, blowing us past what remained of an ancient forest of juniper trees. The dead, twisted, stunted trunks were an agony straight from the mind of Edvard Munch, bearing all the urgency and anger of his figure in 'The Scream'.

Over the next two weeks we drifted in and out of the Tessaout, Bou Wgemmaz, Ait Bouli, Tirsal and Imazane valleys. We trekked hundreds of kilometres and passed through innumerable villages. We camped by rivers, slept in storerooms, rose to sunshine and walked in the rain. We visited a 400-year-old fortified village and climbed over the natural ramparts of far older fortified mountains. Each day we walked, as if along a rainbow, towards a hidden pot of gold. The point where earth met sky in the High Atlas was bountiful with treasure: a special smile, a knowing hug, a silent dawn, a marvellous cloud ... At night the laughter of children and the muttered wisdom of prophets lined the horizon with silver.

It was not without some hesitation that we left such beauty and returned through the looking glass to rendezvous with the *60 Minutes* television crew in mad Marrakesh. The promise of an imminent return was all that made it bearable.

LESOTHO–
KINGDOM IN THE SKY

TIENIE WAS SITTING on his hands, rocking his buttocks from side to side and swinging his white chubby legs back and forth like pendulums. Bold as brass, he announced that he was having a relationship with Azet. They'd been going steady since nursery school, and—'Oh, ask *that* question (why don't you); yes, yes yes ...'—of course they were getting married.

The camera panned to Azet. She was sitting on the desk next to Tienie, her porcelain face a mask of feigned outrage, her mouth sprung like a trap. She did not want to deny the claim, just to show—with a single look—that she was embarrassed to be sharing the intimacies of this most sacred union with strangers. 'I'll slap you one!' she said.

'And where's that? I'll give *you* a slap on the ear!' Tienie retorted. 'Oh no!' cried the damsel, mocking distress. The pair lapsed into a fit of tee-hees and titters.

Lesotho

Malealea

Makhaleng River

Ketenyane River

Semongkong

Ribaneng

Maletsunyane Gorge

Ketane

Thaba Putsoa Range

Masernouse River

Harasvale

Ketane River

Jobo

Maletsunyane River

Ha Nohana

Sengu River

NAMIBIA

BOTSWANA

Swaziland

LESOTHO

Thaba Putsoa

Thabana Ntlenyana

SOUTH AFRICA

It was endearing stuff, if a touch precocious. Azet and Tienie were, after all, just seven years old.

A few more people wandered into the common room where we were watching this sub-titled confession on television. They nodded politely to Chris and me, and settled themselves on the remaining chairs.

It was the only room in the Sani Pass mountain refuge that was even remotely warm—it was already well below zero outside, and the stone dormitories in the crude building were as cold as crypts. The sun was still setting in the west over lofty Lesotho, but its shadow had long been cast upon the embattled province of Natal below. It was so tranquil up here on the edge of the fortifying Drakensberg Escarpment, the thought of rising civil war on the Zulu side of the eyrie chalet seemed totally incomprehensible.

I turned my attention back to Azet and Tienie; they were just warming up. A scene change momentarily placed them in their school assembly, singing the Afrikaners' anthem as the South African flag was being raised. Then we were back in the class-room, listening to more engaging dialogue.

I was halfway through a warm fuzzy giggle when the reporter changed tack and fired off another round of questions. Tienie's answers stopped me dead like bullets.

'What's the main difference between black and white?' the journalist asked. Without even so much as a pause to think it over, the little boy piped, 'I think black people walk around with AK47s more.'

'And what do they do with them?', the reporter asked.

'Shoot each other,' Tienie responded.

Much to my horror, several of my room-mates laughed. An intelligent-looking white[1] teenager sitting right beside me sniggered. He believed that inter-tribal tension would save Afrikaners

---

[1] When I use the term 'whites', unless otherwise specified, I refer to the Afrikaners—who are the descendants of Dutch, French and to a lesser degree German forebears—*and* the English-speaking group.

a veritable fortune on ammunition in the build-up to the nation's first truly democratic—or to use his word—'black' election. His friend agreed, but claimed civilian weaponry was not the answer to all of South Africa's problems: AIDS was. 'The stupid blicks are going to wipe themselves out with it—just you wait and see,' he said. 'AIDS is the true—the only—hope for South Africa now.'

Too shocked to comment, I kept watching the TV.

The pint-sized lovers on the screen were no longer cute and I was no longer smiling at them. They were merely mouthpieces for their parents' prejudices. Their conversation impugned both their age and innocence.

When asked what he would say if they let black children into his rugby team, Tienie's reaction suggested the very idea was too preposterous to even consider. Azet was repulsed by the mere thought of putting black and white together, adding that her mother didn't like blacks at all, and she was not even supposed to *sit* next to (let alone play with) a black boy or girl. It simply wasn't right.

Just when I was starting to think that maybe the interview had preceded the abolition of apartheid, Tienie looked straight down the barrel of the camera and said off-handedly, 'They should never have released that Mandela . . .'

A chorus of agreement echoed around me. I felt ashamed. I wanted to leave the room, but the program was too compelling. I put my hands up to my eyes and continued to watch it, like a horror film, through a veil of fingers.

The program was the first episode in a South African version of the successful British series *Seven Up*. The same cross-section of children appearing in it would be quizzed again when they turned 14, 21 and 28.

Through questions about love, money, crime, politics, school, work and play, the first documentary in the projected series was presenting a poignant portrait, albeit in miniature, of South Africa today. Through the attitudes and aspirations of its impressionable seven-year-old-stars, it was drawing attention to the nation's economic, social and political variances.

Perhaps the most telling comments came from the black and coloured[2] kids, the ones born beyond privilege. Their self-esteem was virtually non-existent. They lived in overcrowded shanty towns on the edges of the cities and in rural villages with communal facilities. Many only saw their parents once a month, as they were forced to live and work away from home.

With the exception of one boy named Katleko, the black kids had a pretty muddled understanding of their own identities and their sense of morality was just as confused as poor Tienie's and Azet's.

For years their communities had been united against a common cause. Side by side they had protested, defying their white oppressors' inequitabe laws. They had joined hands with all manner of groups opposed to apartheid and marched beneath the multiracial banner of the United Democratic Front. Together, they'd organised boycotts and strikes of every description and brought the unpopular rulers of the Republic to their knees. Together, they'd forced an end to racial segregation. Together they'd won the right to vote.

But the way in which they had been governed and controlled for all those years ensured a short-lived honeymoon for the allied revolutionaries. Ethnic rivalry had been accentuated, not suppressed under Afrikaan rule, for three and a half centuries, and now the major tribal groups were abandoning conciliation and confronting one another for future leadership.

It was black against black in South Africa, and the kids in the documentary talked with disarming indifference about watching people kill one another in the streets of their townships and cities. They laughed and bragged about particular eyewitness accounts

---

[2] South African term for people of mixed descent.

as if they were relating favourite scenes from some Itchy and Scratchy cartoon.

The scourge of South Africa was no longer its institutionalised racism, rife as it remained. The new saboteur on the block was tribalism. Katleko called it 'the darkness' but his on-screen peers referred to it more specifically. Depending on their ancestry, the bad guys were either the ANC, Inkatha, Mandela or Buthelezi. Surprisingly, not one of the non-white children even mentioned De Klerk's National Party or the Nazist AWB.[3]

It was apparent, even though the election date had not yet been set, that South Africa was heading for disaster. There were forces that wished to drown democracy in blood; there were factions that wanted to voice their opinions with bullets, not ballots. Freedom would have its price, and if history repeated itself—as it so often did on the African continent—the hard currency would be lives.

As I watched the documentary, I couldn't help but wonder how many of its chance celebrities would be fated for the cross-fire. They stood to lose so much more than the final vestige of their childhood.

Chris and I had been in Southern Africa for the better part of a week, yet this was our first meaningful 'contact' with the issues and realities facing the nation's black majority. There were 27 million of them out there, but the colour of our skin had thus far ensured we only met—and perfunctorily at that—those in service to the whites with whom we fraternised. Apartheid was dead, but its protocol was a long way from the grave yet.

In Johannesburg, we'd been fêted, condemned by our pigmentation to be a party only to white conversations, to feel only white tensions and fears, to eat only white food and enjoy only white forms of entertainment. We moved only through areas settled by whites. To do otherwise was—all things considered—suicidal.

---

[3] Afrikaner Weerstandsbeweging, or in English, the Afrikaner Resistance Movement. Popularly referred to as the 'Afrikaners Without Brains'.

Everyone we met knew someone who had been raped or murdered. Everyone we met *was* someone who had been mugged or burgled.

On the surface Johannesburg resembled any one of a number of Australian cities. There were old sandstone buildings and new glass skyscrapers, malls just like those in Miranda and Bondi, suburbs reminiscent of Double Bay and Chatswood. There were even jacarandas and eucalypts shading the footpaths and late-opening chainstores like 7-11.

But here the similarities ended. There was an atmosphere about the place, a threatening air—real or imagined—that reminded me of the day I'd ventured beyond 42nd Street and Broadway in deepest, darkest New York city.

Walking the streets of Johannesburg was out of the question, having the windows on your car wound down was asking for trouble and carrying a weapon was virtually mandatory. Many of the assistants in shops were holstered, and at the entrance to one of the television studios we visited I had my backpack X-rayed for explosives.

For publicity purposes,[4] and to strengthen the new ties made between South African and Australian sporting interests, we'd agreed to 'do' the media rounds in Johannesburg. Had I been expecting too much too soon in thinking we'd at least get to meet blacks in those public and exalted circles? Alas, we were interviewed exclusively by white radio and television hosts, filmed by white cameramen, photographed by white photographers and questioned only by white reporters.

There were no longer separate buses for blacks and whites—but since the blacks used 'emergency taxis'[5] and the whites drove cars in Johannesburg, repealing the discriminatory rule here had little or no real effect. When you travelled from point A to point

[4] One of our major sponsors, Hi-Tec, was represented in South Africa.
[5] Passenger vehicles, usually combi-vans or Bedfords. Like their cousins—the East African 'matatu' and West African 'mammy-wagons'—they are invariably overcrowded and dilapidated, and driven by B-grade licensed speed-demons.

B, you still didn't have to press flesh or nod off on a shoulder that was a different colour from your own.

People could, by law, live and shop where they chose to now, but very few blacks could yet afford the white lifestyle they aspired to, so the law, in effect, was an ass. You could count the non-whites in the cinemas, restaurants and ritzy malls of the city as easily as you could pick the red sweets out of a box of M and Ms.

Johannesburg—*the whole city*—was what Chinatown or Cabramatta was to Sydney, full-scale. You could enter it and not even know you were in a black country.

It was so bizarre, so unreal. And yet to those who lived there, it made perfect sense. They could not give you answers because in all honesty, they did not understand the questions this madness provoked.

Was I the only one aware of the irony in being asked to check my firearm in the cloakroom before proceeding to the set of *Good Morning South Africa?* With one million AK47's and no-one-knew how many pistols or revolvers reputedly in civilian hands across the country you could understand the reasoning behind the formality, but didn't anyone else in the place find the need for gun-racks instead of umbrella stands in public places just a touch disconcerting? Were we the only people in the city yet to be desensitised to its cruelties? How could we be so naive to suggest emigration as a viable option to white families stalked by fear? Were we so absorbed in what was or wasn't a 'politically correct' ideology to misconstrue the cold hard facts of life?

White South Africans were normal people—like you and me in every respect, save their ethical obligation to mankind. The concept of all men being created equal still seemed inherently implausible to most.

It was early days yet on the road to equal opportunity, but for the time being it was likely the black majority would remain the

Touareg camel traders on their way to markets in Tamanrasset, Algeria.

Goats scrounge for herbage near Ou Edoutoul village in the Hoggar Mountains, Algeria.

Traditional reed enclosure of the Touareg, Ou Edoutoul, Sahara, Algeria.

The vast, desolate Sahara, en route to the Ahaggar Mountains, Algeria.

Chris explores the
surreal world of the
Ahaggar, beneath
Ilamen, Algeria.

A village catches the last sun of the day in the Ounilla valley, Morocco.

The twin lakes of Tamda, Morocco.

Omar Ben Houssain watches over his flock near Imlil, High Atlas, Morocco.

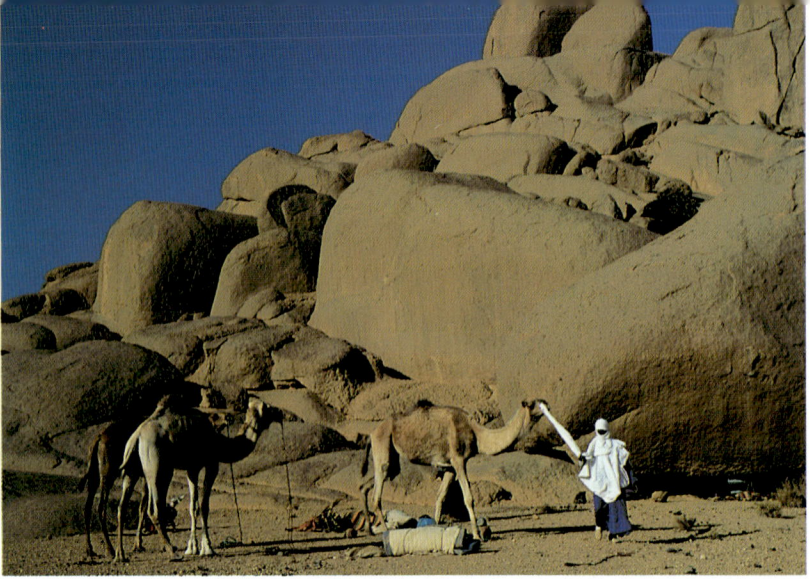

Intakarnet and his camels make camp beneath a boulder pile en route to the Ahaggar Mountains.

Three women from Harasvale, Lesotho, ham it up for the camera.

The magnificent Maletsenyane Gorge, Semomgkong district, Lesotho.

Malehlohono Lo Monyane reading the bones in Malealea village, Lesotho.

Fanroi, Jobo and Sabota from Yorbo village, Lesotho.

Basotho family outside their Rondaval in Ita Nohana village, Lesotho.

nation's second-class citizens: the white minority's 'whipping boy'.

It would have been interesting to have spent more time trying to come to terms with the social and political fabric of modern South Africa. Bruce Haigh, the Canberra-based director of the federally funded Australian South Africa Training Program and former diplomat in South Africa, had furnished me with a list of contacts he felt could prove useful in this regard, but time— and I must admit my own sense of inferiority—kept me from using it. It included people like Bishop Desmond Tutu, the wife of murdered Black Consciousness Movement leader Steve Biko, several lecturers in politics, three former newspaper editors, half a dozen social workers and attorneys, a former detainee on Robben Island, and the Director of the Human Rights Commission in Johannesburg. I wish I'd had the guts to set up at least one meeting, but we were really running late for our appointment with the mountains ...

The *60 Minutes* crew we were supposed to meet up with in Marrakesh during the last week of May had failed to make the rendezvous, sending a fax instead to say they were two weeks behind schedule. By the time they arrived in Morocco and filmed their story, our own climbing agenda was out by a month. The only way we could feasibly put it back on track and keep within Africa's seasonal limitations was by halving our intended stay in the southern end of the continent. If time and confidence permitted, I could look up some of Bruce's contacts at the very end of the expedition, prior to returning to Australia.

In the meantime, however, to be true to the main objective—if not the itinerary—of the African Summit Safari, we planned to climb to the top of the highest peak in the Drakensberg Range, the 3482m Thabana Ntlenyana. It was not far from Sani Pass, where we were now, shielded from the elements by a stone-walled chalet.

It had taken us a full day to reach Sani Pass from Malealea, a village just 84km southeast of Lesotho's capital, Maseru. Public transport was not available to such an obscure destination as this, so Di Jones, co-owner of the lodge and trading store at Malealea, had graciously offered to drive us all the way there and back.

We'd taken the long way around, via the northeastern perimeter or 'Roof of Africa Road', assuming it would be in better condition than the more direct one which crossed the country via the Thaba Putsoa, or 'Blue Mountains', and the Central Maloti Ranges. The last one hundred-odd kilometres, however, had taken four hours to negotiate, so it was anyone's guess whether or not we'd made the right decision.

Lesotho—pronounced Lesutu—was pretty much all mountains whatever way you chose to penetrate it. It was the only country on earth whose total mass rose over the 1500-metre mark.

Thabana Ntlenyana was consequently little more than a disappointing crest in a 'high sea' or plateau of moorland, just five kilometres back from the spectacular tidal-wave wall of the Drakensberg Escarpment. It was so insignificant that the highest point in the whole of Southern Africa had kept itself hidden from the record books for aeons and was only 'discovered' in 1951. The greatest challenge it posed had less to do with mountaineering than it did faith: how were we to know for sure the guide we'd arranged to hire would lead us up the right mountain path?

We needn't have worried. He'd done it all before. We left the chalet early the next morning and by midday we were standing on top of a conical hill marked by a cairn. There was no plaque, just a pile of rocks, but quite clearly it was the highest point in sight.

The climb was nothing to write home about, but the view from the summit was magic, surpassed only by the vista we witnessed back at Sani Pass that evening. Pink springbok clouds leapt across the sky, winter veld turned to rust in the late afternoon light, leaves rained like butterflies from poplar trees and smoke hung like a vapour around the Sani village huts. Dogs barked and horses shied and nightfall set in with a chill.

It was minus 12°C when we set out the following morning to return to Malealea. It dawned on me that prior to planning our African journey, I had never even heard of the Kingdom of Lesotho. The former British protectorate, then known as Basutoland, was a country as easily overlooked in the atlas as its crowning mountain had been from the plateau. Encompassed as it was by the Republic of South Africa, it appeared to be more of a province than an entirely independent state.

Comparable in size to Belgium, it was home to just on two million people. It was one of only three countries in black Africa blessed with ethnic uniformity: 99.7 per cent of the population were Basotho.[6] Although the nation comprised many Sotho clans, they shared the one language, culture and unique historical consciousness. It was, by little coincidence, one of the most peaceful nations on the whole continent, free from the acute tribal rivalry which marked the politics of its neighbour.

If Lesotho's place names were as true to print as its statistics, the Kingdom was not just a Promised Land, it was a credible heaven on earth! On our journey back to Malealea, having chosen the shorter and more direct route, we rollercoasted over a saddle named 'God Help Me Pass' and motored through a gap in the range which was somewhat more reassuringly signposted 'Gates of Paradise'.

We drove past Thaba Bosiu, the 'Mountain of Night', and Di explained how it was even more famous than Thabana Ntlenyana, as it was the celebrated birthplace of the Basotho nation.

In the early 19th century, Southern Africa was besieged by two decades of turmoil. Following the depredations of the great Zulu chieftain Shaka, marauding clans fled across the interior, seeking

---

[6] Lesotho is the name of the country, Basotho or simply Sotho is the name of the people and Sesotho is the name of their language. In all instances, the Os are pronounced as Us and the Hs are silent.

new land and slaying all in their path. Two million people were left dead in their tracks.

A young chief named Mshweshwe[7] gathered the refugees dispersed by the Mfecane (the 'Crushing') and led them into the mountains. Using the natural fortress of the Thaba Bosiu plateau as his base, he beat back invaders and established his people securely against the Zulus. In so doing, he founded the nation of Basotho. Ruling from his impregnable mountaintop, he pursued a policy of peace and prosperity, and although his power waned in the last years of his life the Basotho continue to venerate his name.

Inspired by what we'd seen from our road journey across the breadth of Lesotho, we asked Di's husband Micky to help us devise a trek through some of Malealea's finest hinterland. He determined a route—half of which traversed places never before included on a tourist's itinerary—and set off to find someone in the village who was familiar with that particular distant region. A middle-aged and portly fellow named Tsele assured Micky he knew the way, so despite his reputably abrupt manner, he was hired on as our guide. A younger, gentler and infinitely more handsome man named David was chosen to accompany us as translator and confidant.

The following morning we left Malealea Lodge for a second time. With a trio of ponies in tow, we set off to explore the Thaba Putsoa Range.

It was a staggered start: Tsele had to pick up a few things from the store on his way out, David had to say goodbye to a couple of friends, and Chris and I decided, at the last minute, to visit the local witch doctor.

The 'shaman', much to our surprise, was a beautiful, jowly old woman named Malehlohono lo Monyanengaka. She welcomed us into her spartan mud hut and retrieved her tools of trade from

---

[7] Sometimes spelt Moshoeshoe, also Moshesh. The name Mshweshwe was an imitation of the sounds made by a knife in shaving.

a darkened corner of the room. If it weren't for her headdress of foot-long porcupine quills, her candy-pink frock and civet pelt shawl, she was a dead ringer for Bill Cosby, and could easily have passed herself off as his grandmother.

Malehlohono took her sacred selection of 13 stones, shells and bones from their worn hide pouch and motioned for me to scatter them on the floor, where we were now sitting. The 'bones', as they were collectively and popularly called, had passed through the generations—along with 'the power'—and with them Malehlohono was able to divine our future fortunes.

After a few minutes summoning assistance from both her ancestors and the Almighty, she proceeded to decode the final alignment of the 13 objects. With a smile sparkling in her eyes and a lilt in her gentle voice, she promised us—through an interpreter—that our whole expedition in Africa would be a success. We would come to no harm. Our marriage was great, our health was perfect, we were strong and happy and would always have plenty of money and luck. There were no bad omens, only good ones: so Halleluiah, Praise the Lord, hallowed be thy name!

She closed the session with a second muttered prayer.

Like many African nations, the Basotho combined their traditional beliefs and practices with introduced religious dogma. It was perfectly acceptable in West Africa, for example, to pursue Catholicism and voodooism concurrently, even though to puritanical outsiders the two were so ostensibly opposed. In the north, Sunni Moslem Berbers prayed to Allah, yet—in spite of strong protest from Koranic scholars abroad—they continued to frequent the *koubbas,* or tombs, of miracle healers and seek consultation from *marabouts* for infertility, eye ailments and psychological disorders.

Here in the south, the Basotho incorporated the best of both worlds as well, praising the Lord in one and the same breath as calling on the spirits of departed ancestors for guidance. They read their bibles, but they also sacrificed livestock from time to time in propitiation of ancestral wrath or in anticipation of good fortune for the family. Their pagan customs were tolerated, but not condoned by any of the official churches.

I couldn't help but wonder what the African continent would be like today, had governments sought to apply the same eclectic principles used to shape their spiritual identities, to reform their politics; to attain what, for many, had proved an elusive sense of nationhood.

Missionaries had been a part of the scene in Lesotho since 1833, no more than half a dozen years after the actual inception of the Kingdom. Mshweshwe encouraged the activities of his first 'clothed' crusaders without personally accepting their doctrine, but today 90 per cent of his followers' descendants counted themselves as members of the great Christian family. Half of them were Roman Catholic and the rest were Protestant, most subscribing to the home-grown creed of the Lesotho Evangelical Church.

We said goodbye to Malehlohono and with her blessing, began our journey in earnest. The odd couple were riding, Chris and I were walking and half a dozen children were tagging behind, singing as they frolicked like seagulls in the wake of our departure. Their luminous harmonies were as natural and free and open as their faces. It was music straight from heaven, and even though the only English phrase used in the rendition was 'Two by two', it was repeated often enough to make clear the song was a Sunday School favourite. Noah would have been impressed.

It was a beautiful crisp winter's morning; the sky was a deep cerulean, the earth, Centre-red. A gentle breeze whispered to the last ears of maize in the fields and people came out from their homes to greet us as we passed.

We followed a trail down the side of the deeply cut Makhaleng Valley, crossed its cold, clear river and trekked up the other side to David's mother's village at the foot of the Thaba Putsoa Range.

Chris just couldn't seem to share my enthusiasm for the scenery, for the sweeping rural views and mountain-lined horizons. Once again, his eyes were firmly fixed to the trail: it was absolutely littered with crystal quartz and bejewelled fragments of long broken thunder-eggs. The ground was this man's oyster, and in it he was determined to find me a pearl ...

After lunch we wandered along the Ribaneng Valley. Giant aloe plants lined the route, and formed living kraals for livestock behind each cluster of dwellings. It was so peaceful we could hear the tinkling of cow bells from at least 500 metres—maybe even a kilometre—away.

The further we trekked from the road-linked Malealea, the more traditional and picturesque the village buildings became— squat, cylindrical huts with conical thatched roofs known as ron- davels, made of mud, dung and perfectly trimmed and layered straw. To express individuality, patterns had been worked into the brilliant ochre rendering of the exteriors while they were still moist. Periodically house-proud mamas resurfaced the floors of their homes with fresh dark olive dung. Once dry, it formed a hard dust-resistant plaster over the earthen foundation. Sprinkling it with water each day after sweeping stopped it from cracking prematurely.

We arrived in the tiered village of Ribaneng just after 4pm. Several men in the top family 'compound' where we were destined to stay were busy breaking the sun-dried kernels from a huge pile of maize cobs. Their wives, each with a sleeping rag-doll-limp baby tied by a blanket to her back, were winnowing stray bits of husk from the grain. Older children were playing at their feet in the falling 'snow'. A locally made tape of rhythmic praise-songs, performed by the Maseru Voice Waves choir, was playing on a ghetto-blaster, but the melody of conversation prompted by our arrival soon rose above it.

As the sun disappeared over the mountains, out came the blan- kets, the distinctive Basotho cloak which—when topped with a funnel-shaped woven grass lampshade—pretty well constituted the national costume. Kids wore thin checked tasselled rugs, folded in half, and their parents wore nice thick wraps, patterned with regal-looking motifs of crowns, crests, seals, crossed staves, trefoils, and heraldic *fleurs de lis*.

Chris and I bedded down in the rondavel reserved for guests. David and Tsele disappeared after dusk to lodge with friends. Using the dried de-kernelled cobs as firewood, mothers set about the business of cooking the family's evening share of maizemeal porridge. The air was rich with the smell of smoke and the low murmur of voices, muffled behind closed doors. Silence fell like a lullaby over the village and rocked its children to sleep.

In the morning we woke to find a lithe 11-year-old boy sitting on our doorstep, wearing nothing but a blanket, a pair of thread-bare undies and long white gumboots. He'd come to take us on a side trip up to Ribaneng Falls. Forgoing breakfast, we followed him into the shadowed folds of the mountains directly behind the village, and disappeared into another world entirely.

We swished through the thick dry grasses of the veld, then slipped quietly into an ever-narrowing kloof. The ground was laden with the fallen leaves of autumn; the bare branches laced the remnant of blue sky overhead. We zigzagged across a stream, slipping and sliding from rock to bank and before long reached the end of the ravine.

Water gushed from the lip of the terminating chamber. The 50-metre face behind the fall was heavily glazed with verglas and icicles hung from its sideburn whiskers of grass. The downdraft, almost strong enough to lean on, was colder than the breath of death.

The pool below the cascade was frozen solid and beads of ice dislodged by its force ran across the surface, like unstrung pearls falling on a polished marble floor. The tumult of the torrent reverberated against the walls enclosing it and filled the vale with anger.

For a relatively small drop, the might of Ribaneng was pretty fearsome. Within seconds we were snap-frozen; within minutes, deafened. Our twiggy guide had the good sense to retreat, but we stayed in the coldroom for half an hour, filming.

It took the whole return journey to thaw out. Young David had the packhorse readied for loading and his own mount watered and saddled. Tsele was stuffing his face—something he seemed to do almost continuously—and his poor undernourished horse was chafing at the bit to get the day's torture under way. Not wanting to upset the applecart, Chris and I quickly packed up our kit and, empty-tummied, headed off for distant Ketane.

We crossed the Thaba Putsoa range at midday. The top of the plateau was a mass of red-hot poker plants, which must have made for a magnificent vista in spring when their thrusting stems were aglow with flowers. The lee-side of the weathered battlements jutting out from the ridge were streaked with drifts of crystalline snow, the first of winter's fall. The air was so fresh we drank it like a tonic.

Herd boys, with cheeks aflush and white teeth flashing, raced away from their cow-watching posts to see what strange creatures were blowing in on the wind. They were a handsome breed, with more responsibility than their years bespoke. Many in their tender teens assumed paternal roles, as their fathers were forced to seek employment far away from the family fold.

Lesotho, beautiful as it seemed, was sadly lacking in resources. In order to make ends meet, nearly half the nation's able-bodied men were obliged to live and work under a pernicious migrant labour system in South Africa. The consequences were often dire on the domestic front, completely disrupting the social and economic life of many villagers.

The women of Lesotho were resolute, but living apart from their menfolk for repetitive periods of indefinite length put a strain on many of their marriages. As if rearing one's youngest children single-handedly wasn't taxing enough, they had to plan their family budgets with, at best, unpredictable resources and, perhaps, differing priorities from their missing husbands. Come

October, tensions would peak as the task of ploughing made the absence of their partners even more hard-felt.

Things looked grim from the women's perspective, but the life their men led away from home was hardly enviable. The next day, having reached the village of Semongkong on the far side of the rollicking plateau that extended between the Ketenyane and Maletsunyane Rivers, we met a retired man named Thabo Mokhanya. He asked us to stay the night with his family, and after dinner he described what it had been like working on and off in South Africa.

Like many of his kinsfolk, he had toiled in the gold and diamond mines of Transvaal and Orange Free State. The industry had always been organised along racial lines, so the unskilled and badly paid jobs were the lot of non-whites. Forty-two South African cents a day, or 14 Rand[8] a month, was all Thabo could hope to earn as he laboured his way through the 1970s. He was barely able to feed his family, let alone save for their future, on such a meagre wage.

The nominal pay Thabo pocketed reflected the conscious and systematic efforts by the government of the day to control black labour and channel it to the benefit of whites. 'It was shameful for me to be away from my family for so long and for so little money,' Thabo confided quietly, his eyes cast. 'It is my disgrace. But we had no choice.'

As if it wasn't bad enough being separated from their families for long periods at a time, imagine how many of Thabo's colleagues felt when they returned home to find their wives pregnant, or nursing an illegitimate babe in arms. They were compliant, but it must have caused them untold sorrow.

The next morning we left Semongkong early. A rich balm of smouldering dung hugged the ground like a river mist and frost crunched like gravel underfoot.

---

[8] At the time of our visit, one Rand was worth about 48 Australian cents.

We followed David and Tsele over to the rim of the Maletsun-yane Gorge. We were not expecting much from this supposed wonder; the lay of the land in these parts seemed pretty nondescript and unyielding. The featureless highland veld seemed to stretch forever.

Suddenly a giant crack appeared. The ground just fell away, several hundred metres beneath our feet. We were standing on the edge of an awesome chasm, as wide as it was deep, staring down into the very bowels of the earth.

The western wall of the ancient sandstone gorge was drenched in sunshine, but the river bed below was still as black as night. Shafts of light, like arrows from the bow of morning, pierced the deep blue void between. Water tumbled, roaring, screaming, falling down some shadowed, hidden face, and filled the air with thunder.

The energy, the light, the sheer enormity of the scene suffused me completely. My soul ached with the burden of its beauty.

We could not see any readily negotiable track or route straight down into the gorge. Thwarting our hopes of standing at the foot of the waterfall heading the Maletsunyane—the largest single-drop in Africa—Tsele insisted the only descent suitable for horses lay beyond the village of Harasvale, a dozen-odd kilometres due south of Semongkong.

Falling into step behind our guide, we headed across the plateau. Under the circumstances, it was difficult to register dis-appointment: the sheer magnificence of our 'aerial' view of the gorge well surpassed our desire to explore its shadowy depths. We were still talking about it when we hit the last hamlet on the highland, several hours later.

Nine men were standing shoulder to shoulder in a line on the edge of the Harasvale fields, manually breaking kernels from a pile of sun-dried cobs. Marking time with the strains of a praise-song, they raised crude wooden mallets high over their heads and brought them down in unison on the maize. Steady as a heartbeat, they pounded and sweated and sang, the rhythm of life pulsing from their veins to the earth.

Everything about the scene was idyllic, a perfect cameo of rural harmony, and Chris quickly set up the video to film it. The sun was not yet directly overhead, and a dozen backlit horses cantered through the stubbled fields. Children ran behind them, effervescent with laughter. Before long, half a dozen voluptuous mamas swayed into view, balancing buckets of home brew and steaming pots of maizemeal and spinach on their heads.

We were a welcome—if surprise—distraction from the norm. Affecting an entirely non-verbal greeting, the women got down on their knees, unbuttoned their shirts and shook their melon-breasts right in front of a very blushed and slightly flabbergasted Chris. They laughed and teased him with their ample sex, and presented him with a two-litre can of beer.

We were told to help ourselves to the food, but Chris, David and I sensed there wasn't really enough to go around and declined the gracious offer. Tsele knew no such decorum and hogged into it with both hands. Before the workers even got a look-in he'd wolfed down half of their repast.

Embarrassed by his gluttony, we searched our packs for a suitable form of compensation. Chris passed around a few packets of cigarettes and I relinquished our own meagre lunch to the cause. Worried that Tsele would continue to binge as long as we lingered, we quickly but reluctantly packed up the video and headed off to find the downward trail.

The guy was a social liability. Any efforts we made to bridge the gap between black and white were cancelled by his insensitive, self-important behaviour. He was using us as an excuse to abuse the tradition of Lesotho hospitality. Apparently Tsele had not asked whether we could bed-down or camp in particular villages—he had insisted people make room for his charges. His attitude no doubt reflected badly on us, and that made me very angry. What was worse, the premise on which he'd been employed as our guide was entirely false. He didn't know the way at all, and was constantly seeking directions from every man, woman and child we passed, begging for edible handouts as well as advice.

We trekked for the rest of the day without stopping, lest he cause us further grief, and reached the large village of Jobo just on nightfall. The chief had left for Maseru the day before, but his wife—Mabakuena Jobo Lerotholi—took us in regardless.

Mabakuena, who spoke English fluently, confirmed Tsele's anticipated bungling of the situation, but said it had nothing to do with us. 'It is the male African way,' she maintained. 'They just turn up here with nothing, no food, no blankets, and expect us to look after them.'

Since we were the first white tourists to visit Jobo for many years, we tried our best to undo the ill-will of our presumptuous guide and spent a really lovely evening talking to our hostess.

Mabakuena led a comparatively privileged life. As wife of the headman, she would never want for anything. Her own father had been a chief, and conforming to a time-honoured strategy which perpetuated domination of his clan, he had married her off to one of his own junior kinsmen. By tradition, the chiefs of Lesotho held the prerogative of allocating arable land to their subjects and controlled the distribution of cattle, so marriages within 'the family' were both economically and politically advantageous, capable of creating powerful factional alliances.

The only thing missing from Mabakuena's life was children. In a society which celebrated motherhood as the fulfilment of a woman's true role in the social order, her barrenness was regarded as a tragic condition.

Mabakuena was not without surrogates, though, and a steady stream of waifs played around her home and compound throughout the evening. Several slept over, sharing a patch of floor-space with a freshly slaughtered carcass, a pile of saddle cloths and two very long, very thin and very white aliens from Australia.

We spent a few days exploring the area between the Maletsunyane, Ketane and Sengu Rivers, then climbed back up into the
snow-dusted realm of the Thaba Putsoa foothills. The weather
was so abysmal on our second-last day on the trail, we had to
abandon our attempt to re-cross the range and subsequently spent
most of the time huddled over a charcoal and dung fire inside a
cosy, smoke-filled rondavel.

On our host's short-wave radio, we caught the news that the
World Trade Centre just outside Johannesburg was under siege.
White separatists from the Conservative Party and the Afrikaner
People's Front had gathered there to protest the June 24th decision *not* to create a white homeland in South Africa. Members of
the militant AWB arrived on the scene and stormed the Conven-
tion Hall, where several leading politicians were holding crucial
negotiations on the future government of South Africa. They
occupied the chamber for three hours, harassing delegates and
vandalising the building.

While De Klerk and his National Party were willing to
empower the black majority and relinquish their control of the
country, the right-wing extremists were clearly not prepared to
give in so easily. The loyalty of the predominantly white security
forces was thrown into question when the 600 police guarding
the building made no effort whatsoever to repel the invaders.

I am sure I was not alone in wondering how different the consequences may have been, had the protesters causing the disrup-
tion been black. Bullets would have surely flown and those left
standing would have been arrested—but because the assailants
were white, the uniformed officers held their fire. Only one man
was charged—with illegal parking—after he'd crashed his truck
through the plate-glass doors of the centre.

It was a bleak old day outside, and my mood reflected it
accordingly. With the news at hand, I was soon engulfed by what
young Katleko from the *Seven Up South Africa* program had
called 'the darkness'.

It would hang like a cloud over me for week, fuelled by thoughts and uncertainties over South Africa's fate. It would follow me back to Johannesburg and beyond. All I could do was hope and pray for sunshine.

The end of apartheid would see the creation of a new country— a new constitution, a new flag, a new anthem and above all else, a new ethos. But would an all-race election bring an end to the nation's problems, or herald a start to new nightmares?

Apartheid was not only a political system, but an economic one as well. How quickly would the new government be able to meet the ultimate promise of political freedom with equal economic opportunity? How would they get the $142-billion per annum economy working in the interest of *all* South Africans? Would they find an equitable solution *of their own,* one that would not cause further problems of massive hardship, lower living standards and loss of production?

I wanted so much to believe the new nation would provide an economic awakening for greater Black Africa; that it would be the engine to pull the continent from its mire of poverty and desperation; that it would become, as Archbishop Tutu predestined, 'a paradigm for the rest of the world'. But I just couldn't shake the fear that it would all fall apart—that the martial history of the Zulus or the vow of white extremist groups to wage 'a war of resistance' would lead inevitably to bloodshed, if not civil war.

Success would surely go a long way towards offsetting the dismal record of failure that blights the rest of black-ruled Africa, but how realistic was its attainment? Only God knew. Only time would tell.

We left Johannesburg with more questions and fewer answers ... with great regret, but little hope.

Never had a place left me feeling so damn cheerless.

IDI AMIN AND THE
MOUNTAINS OF THE MOON

ONLY IN THE air was it possible to forget, to dismiss the torment and remember the vision. To dream. For a few hours I could float like a helium balloon, carried on a current of illusion and relief, far away from the troubled earth, with nothing but space before and inside me. I could close my eyes and block out the pain. For a few hours, I could breathe without choking on stones of sadness and fear.

From 10 000 metres, Africa was once again sublime, a paean of beauty, a rhapsody of light. It was everything you ever wanted to believe it to be: a perfume, a tonic, a song. It was the vast endless plain, the boundless sky. It was a landscape that 'had not its like in all the world'.[1] It was omnipotent; absolute.

At 10 000 metres, it was easy to lose one's self in the stereotype, to give one's self up to the motion-picture myth. If Chris

---

[1] A quote from Karen Blixen's *Out of Africa*.

Uganda

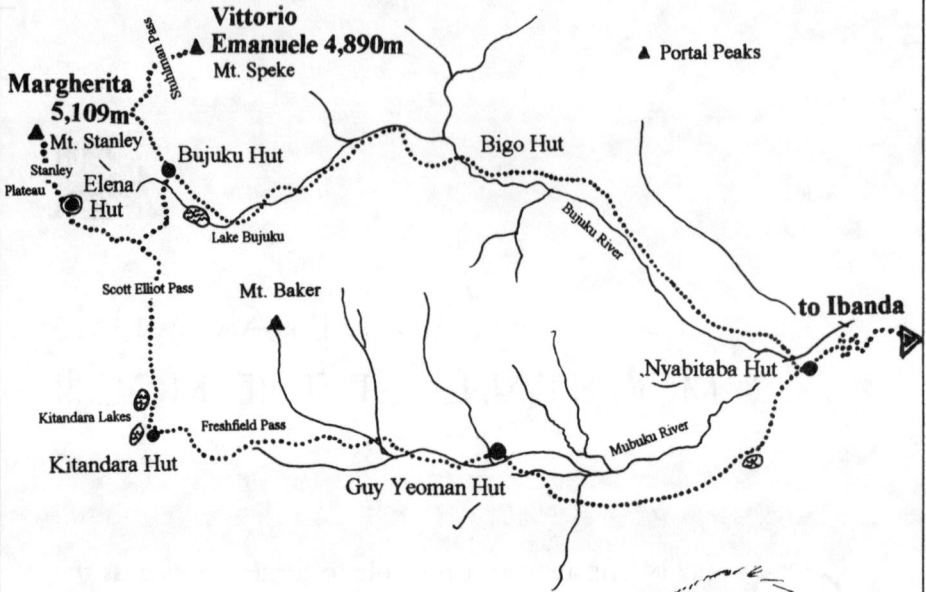

Margherita
5,109m
▲ Mt. Stanley

Stanley
Plateau

◉ Elena
Hut

Sultman Pass

Vittorio
Emanuele 4,890m
Mt. Speke

▲ Portal Peaks

● Bujuku Hut

Bigo Hut

Lake Bujuku

Bujuku River

Scott Elliot Pass

Mt. Baker
▲

to Ibanda ▷

Nyabitaba Hut ●

Kitandara Lakes

Freshfield Pass

Mubuku River

Kitandara Hut ●

Guy Yeoman Hut ●

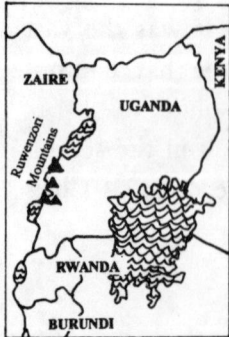

ZAIRE

UGANDA

KENYA

Ruwenzori Mountains

RWANDA

BURUNDI

were Clark Gable, if I were the Twisties girl, perhaps we could have vanished into MGM's *Mogambo* forever.

Within minutes of landing at Nairobi's Kenyatta Airport, I realised I was not the only one smitten by Afrifiction-fever. By comparison, in fact, I barely had a temperature. The arrival hall was febrile with look-alike Redfords and Pecks, would-be Gardners and heavily accented Streeps. We were surrounded by a pining herd of safari suits and pith helmets.

Every second middle-aged or latter-day tourist was wearing a pair of clean-cut fawn trousers or shorts and a manilla-hue shirt with epaulets, a fashion statement as crass as the advertising which idealised it. It was the sort of quasi-military clothing that looked sharp enough on the rack back home, but here—*in situ*, as it were—it was nothing short of a howling *faux pas*. More *haut cliché* than *haute couture*. I couldn't help but imagine these same people decking themselves out in Hawaiian shirts for their annual vacation in Honolulu, or wearing the whole damn cowboy-catastrophe on a business trip to Texas.

Out of Africa and its forerunners were not just culpable for immortalising a genre of clothing—they were responsible for the very presence of at least half the travellers queuing now in front of me at the customs counter. They were glorifying, nostalgic films, powerful anachronisms which perpetuated an entire tourism industry, eternalising Africa's romantic lore. And somehow our infatuation with their opiate myth justified our ignorance of modern black Africa. Perhaps it was easier to just accept the delusion than attempt to fathom the truth.

Thanks to Hollywood, Kenya's current and future status as the safari capital of the continent was assured. People came from all over the world to stalk wild animals and trophy their 'kills' in brag-books and coffee-table albums. They were modern-day hunters, armed to the hilt with SLRs and 100 ASA ammunition, and they arrived in their tens of thousands each week. Collectively they contributed upwards of half-a-billion dollars to the national coffers per annum.

Chris and I would not be touring the inescapable Kenyan safari circuit just yet; we were only stopping temporarily in Nairobi, *en route* to neighbouring Uganda. This time around, we were merely picking up provisions and equipment we had earlier air-freighted from Australia, and establishing a sort of 'supply depot' for the remainder of the expedition.

Nairobi was the obvious choice for such a base camp. It was the hub, to all intents and purposes, of East Africa. Our major sponsors, Data General, were represented there and Australia had established its East African diplomatic mission in the city. Paul Cameron, the High Commission's Technical Attaché-cum-resident mountaineer, had enthusiastically offered to help Chris and me with logistics and accommodation. He was currently fixing phones in South Africa, so accepting a second offer we'd had from close friends of Bruce Haigh's, we caught a taxi out to Anthony and Jenny Hawkes' home in Langata, a semi-rural suburb adjoining the huge Nairobi National Park.

Jenny had just bought a 'faaarm in Affreeka at the foot of the Ngong Hills'; Anthony was squatting for his tennis coaching exams. Their two kids were finishing the term at the local International School then transferring to elite boarding schools in London: a perk of Anthony's position as Consular General for the British High Commission.

The whole family were having an affair with Africa, specifically Kenya; it was something you felt immediately, and knew that it would always be so. On our first night with them we listened to stories of fabulous parties held in the old art-deco Ricciadi[2] residence on the shores of Lake Naivasha. We looked at photos of a million flamingoes feeding on algae in Lake Natron. The kids told us how they ate flying ants, captured mid-flight and consumed by

[2] The Ricciadis were celebrated pioneering adventurers who settled in Kenya.

the handful, and spoke of adventures more fantastic than anything I could recall having seen as a child on Marlon Perkins' *Animal Kingdom*.

Slipping into conversation as readily as conjunctives were the names of Kenya's leading conservationists. The recent plane crash and imminent amputation of Richard Leakey's[3] leg came up, as did the ongoing efforts of elephant-experts Iain and Oria Douglas-Hamilton and Cynthia Moss. They were all personal friends of the Hawkes and talk of their activities brought to life the stories I'd so often read about them in magazines.

Anthony told us about the plight of people deserting their villages for the promise of the big smoke, about murders and crimes symptomatic of the ensuing social and urban decay. We discussed local politics, unemployment, ideology and tribalism. The tone was never patronising or paternalistic and disparagement was constructive rather than racist in its intent.

The Hawkes' introduction into Kenya was unparalleled, and we would always be grateful to them for it. It was largely an expatriate view, but one on which we could build, slowly but assuredly, some kind of understanding of the nation at large.

Chris and I spent a few days in Langata, writing postcards, reading and planning the first of our East African climbs. A day and a half, two bribes and twenty-three signatures later, we completed the customs procedures necessary to repossess our air-freighted supplies, and put them safely into storage. The next morning we applied for our Ugandan visas and bought tickets on the overnight bus to Kampala.

I could barely contain the excitement I felt at the prospect of reaching our ultimate destination in Uganda. Of all the peaks we intended climbing on this journey, the fabled 'Mountains of the Moon' would doubtlessly prove second to none. They actually

---

[3] The celebrated anthropologist and critic-turned-director of Kenya Wildlife Service.

comprised the range around which I'd constructed the whole premise of our expedition.

When Chris first suggested Africa, in 1992, my initial reaction had been to plan something along the banks of the Nile. Anxious for a 'hook' on which to hang the venture, I figured we could re-walk the path of some or one of the great African explorers: John Hanning Speke, Richard Burton, David Livingstone or Henry Morton Stanley. I pulled out the atlas and began tracing my finger along the course of the longest river on the face of the earth, starting at its delta on the Mediterranean.

Egypt had always fascinated me. Pictures of the pyramids and street scenes of Cairo were the first to leap from the pages of an old dog-eared *National Geographic* magazine the day I discovered it in a friend's garage. I was 11 and I could scarcely believe they were real—that places like that existed beyond my twin realms of fantasia and suburbia. Those photographs were the catalyst for what I was essentially doing with my adult life, and studying the map brought back all the thrill and wonder I'd felt 20 years ago, squatting down on my pre-pubescent haunches, in a pile of for-gotten possessions and dust.

My eyes scanned the vast tracts of yellowed land on either side of the snaking blue line and in my mind, I conjured images to suit the terrain. The areas were mapped in accordance to the predom-inant tribe peopling them—the Nubians, Dongola, Dinka and Nuer—and I tried to remember what I'd seen and read of their cultures.

When my finger reached Lake Albert and my eyes focused on the small print etched between the contours of the Zaire-Uganda border, I felt my heart skip a beat. It was the source, not the extent of the serpentine river that impassioned the thirty-one-year-old me; it was no longer the man-made mountains built by the pharaohs which caused my pulse to race, but the real snow-and ice-covered ones—their mirror image at the far end of the river.

And now, not even so much as a year later, we were actually on our way there!

We passed through the border town of Malaba shortly before sunrise. Pedlars and black marketeers were already on the make, setting up shop on the Kenyan and Ugandan sides of the border, or touting as they walked to and fro across the no-man's land between. A gaggle of scrawny six- and seven-year-old urchins hawked hard-boiled eggs and sodas. Plump mamas swathed in bolts of vivid screen-printed cotton flogged bananas. Men in their early twenties ran the no-nonsense illegal money exchange. The transactions were lightning fast, with great wads of notes as thick as a thesaurus changing hands every few seconds. Despite the hour, there were people everywhere and a kilometre-long line of trucks, fully loaded with imports, was waiting for the Ugandan customs officer to show up before proceeding to Kampala.

Our bus was back on the road just after 7am, hurtling along through a vision of fertility and splendour. As far as the eye could see, the land was green, smothered in banana plantations, sugar cane and finger millet. Sunflowers grew around roadside villages and thousands of stunning yellow and black napoleon weavers flocked and twittered in and out of spherical nests, dripping like Christmas baubles from the lush foliage of an occasional candelabra tree.

Not far from the border we were stopped by military police. Everyone filed off the bus, walked past the soldiers, and settled themselves on benches in the shade. Chris and I just followed the local lead—it was obvious from the way everyone was behaving that the stop would be a lengthy one. A couple of uniforms sauntered onto the bus and started opening bags at random, pulling them from luggage racks, or scooping them up from passengers' seats.

Exactly what the soldiers hoped to find was never made clear; they were in all likelihood just carrying out a routine search for no other reason save a bit of muscle-flexing. Amazing what an oath and an insignia—not to mention a gun—will do to a man ...

The inspection and scrutiny of passports took an hour, and five minutes into the resumed journey we were stopped again by a second unit, for a second search. Their manner was a little more menacing, and judging by the piles of obviously confiscated or back-handed boxes of goods they had stashed in the thatched huts of their makeshift compound, their approach was good for business too. I watched in amazement as one khaki-clad sleaze pocketed a bottle of perfume from a young woman's handbag. She didn't even flinch—in fact, she looked the other way as if nothing was happening.

I suppose she, and other such victims of intimidation and coercion, were thankful to escape such confrontations with their lives. What was a spray-pack of cologne or a crate of soft-drink worth, anyway? A few years ago a similar encounter would have certainly ended in rape, torture or murder. A simple fleecing was nothing to a people so used to abuse they'd forgotten how to respond to it appropriately.

The woman now without her perfume was roughly my age. She was probably born just in time to see, but not remember, independence. As I was coming to grips with toilet training and marvelling at the Mouseketeers, she was watching the promise of freedom disintegrate right before her sparkling innocent eyes. As Obote, the hard-drinking tyrant elected to rule the new nation, set about abolishing parliament, nationalising the economy, destroying the Buganda monarchy and establishing a one-party state, my own country was being reshaped by two entirely positive forces: affluence and immigration. A hundred thousand Europeans a year were flocking to 'the lucky country' to share the bounty.

When I was bounding around a Victaed lawn on my space-hopper wearing hot-pants and discovering boys, the woman without perfume was witnessing the start of Idi Amin's reign of terror: watching the systematic elimination of her country's intelligentsia, the expulsion of its 72 000 Asians and the wholesale slaughter of entire villages populated by Obote-supporters. The year I came of age was the year Amin was forced into exile in Libya. Some 300 000 Ugandans were dead. The nation was destroyed.

I went to college and learnt how to stand up for my rights, how to be independent, how to love. The woman without perfume was learning how to turn a blind eye and keep her mouth shut, how to steal to survive, how not to hold anyone too dear, lest they be taken from you in the dead of night. Chaos gave way to anarchy. Obote returned to the presidential chair by means of a rigged election.

In the time it took me to drop out of art school, free-wheel 17 000 kilometres across Asia and trek right across Tibet, more than a million Ugandans were displaced and a further 500 000 massacred. Most had been tortured before they were clubbed to death; what little flesh they had on their limbs had been hacked off to the bone ... children had been forced to bite off, chew and swallow each other's noses ... women by the score had been sexually violated, their breasts cut off, their buttocks barbequed, their vaginas pierced by red-hot pokers.

Museveni and his National Resistance Army, aiming to reconstruct the nation democratically, seized leadership in 1986. Since then the lot of the Ugandan citizen had improved enormously, but human rights violations, including the torture of civilians by security forces, persisted. Despite a pledge to hold general elections and a referendum before 1990, the country was still ruled by its transitional military regime. President Museveni's protracted period of nation wide 'rehabilitation and convalescence' continued, the revival of political parties was still deemed divisive, and party activities would remain suspended until completion of the on-going constitution-making process.

The woman without perfume had celebrated her 30th birthday

in peace, but how many of her friends had missed the party? The new spectre stalking the country was AIDS, and it was wiping out men, women and children with even less discretion than Amin and Obote. What small consolation and comfort the populace had found in physical contact with one another had been nothing short of suicidal. Informed sources estimated that 1.5 million Ugandans are HIV positive: 8 per cent of the rural population and between 20 and 30 per cent of the country's urban citizens.[4]

What troubled me most was the resigned acceptance, both within Africa and beyond, of not only Uganda's fate, but that of post-colonial black Africa in general. The atrocities of Amin and Obote, the methodical eradication of 100 000 Tutsis in Rwanda, the annihilation of 200 000 Hutus in Burundi, the destruction of Equatorial Guinea at the hands of President-for-life Macias Nguemna Biyogo . . . the list went on and on, on a par with—if not worse than—the extermination of the Jews by the Nazis, and yet each incident was merely a footnote in history.

When they weren't dying because of despotism or tribalism, Africans were invariably the victims of our world's worst natural disasters: floods, droughts, famines, plagues and epidemics. Many nations had become welfare states, their survival dependent on the whims of foreign donors and aid agencies. Almost daily, for all my adult life, I had been shown footage of starving Ethiopians, Sudanese or Somalians and black-and-white advertisements beseeching freedom from hunger. Almost daily, I'd been asked to put my hand in my pocket for Africa.

Well, now I had my feet on her soil, my eyes glued to her horizon, and my hand nowhere near my wallet: it was holding onto my chest, for fear of having my heart ripped right out of it with grief. I honestly thought I'd been rendered immune to tears by over-exposure to Africa's nightmares. All it had taken to open the floodgates this time around, was one damn bottle of perfume.

[4] Ugandan AIDS Commission, reported by Associated Press on 29th March, 1993.

It didn't help to pity. It didn't help to criticise. How the hell was I ever going to find any answers when trained experts and advisers had so obviously failed to do so? Forget answers—how would I even come to terms with the questions? The despair? As much as I hate to admit it, part of me really envied the supervised safari-suited set, looking at animals all day with a pair of blinkers or blinders on their bridles, oblivious to the real issues of Africa. Tracking spoor and compiling species lists had to be less traumatising and stressful than actually thinking about people and tallying the abominations which had led to their demise.

We reached Kampala at midday. The humidity was as oppressive as the history, and just as visible. It hung like a pall over the buildings. For want of funds, little had been done to restore the broken capital to its former glory. Once described 'a fairytale' by Winston Churchill, Kampala, caught in the cross-fire of misrule and civil war, was a city falling apart, even as it tried to pull itself together. Windows were missing in quantity from office blocks, the streets were cratered with massive potholes and teeming with open sewerage and refuse, electricity and water were at best sporadic in their supply. It was business as usual in the restaurants and cafes, and store shelves were well stacked with an odd but abundant assortment of merchandise.

It surprised me to learn that many of the expelled Indian and Pakistani shopkeepers had returned to redominate the commercial sector of Kampala. The grandchildren of Britain's 'coolie labour force'—responsible for the Mombasa/Kampala railway—had put aside the past in an effort to help rebuild the future. No matter how great the resentment of their presence had been, they still called Kampala home and, with true Asian prudence, had reseized the bull of opportunity by the horns. They knew they would never be recompensed for the $2000-million booty they'd been forced to leave behind in 1972, but since their investment in the country went well beyond the monetary, they were willing to give Uganda another go.

More amazing still was the obvious fact that Ugandans were prepared to take that same second chance. The light that shone within them was something I did not expect to see. Yes, there was resignation, a patience that many would perceive to be apathy, but in spite of everything, there was genuine *joie de vivre* as well. The light was radiant, like a sanctuary lamp burning in a Catholic church. There was something far stronger than faith in the heart of these people; though continuously battered, their values endured.

If not the true hope for Africa, it was at least enough to inspire and raise my own spirits. As long as Ugandans could still tell jokes and laugh and give each other so much more than just the time of day, there was occasion to believe in a future. And that in itself was due reason to relax and enjoy, to look past the broken pipes and shot-out windows, to see beyond that wretched third dimension.

Chris and I spent the afternoon talking to people: to the young staff attending the reception desk at the budget hotel we booked into, to two businesswomen lunching in a popular cafe, to a teller at the bank, the new owner of a Chinese restaurant and a woman selling newspapers on the street. All of them welcomed us to Uganda and each went out of his or her way to share their collective optimism—not their misery—with us.

An Egyptian circus was in town, so we treated ourselves to a unique evening's entertainment. Substantially patronised by expatriates and Asians, the travelling show was clearly a family affair with every member of the clan taking part in no fewer than three acts. Gone were the death-defying feats and crotch-splitting costumes synonymous with a Big Top in the West; these guys and gals were all lard and lubber, not sequins and savvy, and their star performances came from Mr Tubby the tight-rope walker and the sexy Snake Siren—who absolutely stole the show by tongue-kissing a three-metre python.

Before sunrise the next day we were down at the bus station, hunting out the vehicle which would carry us to Kasese. There were hundreds of run-down buses and *matatus* parked end-to-end and side by side in a field of mud and rubbish; the chaos more reminiscent of a scrap-metal heap than a transport depot. Thousands of intending passengers, bleary-eyed and bewildered, searched in the darkness for licence-plate numbers to match those scrawled on their tickets. If there was any semblance of order in the mayhem, it was known only to the street boys, who—with the kind of entrepreneurial effrontery we'd come to expect from the Third World—had made it their business to assist wayward commuters through the mechanical maze. For a few *shillingi mia mojas*,[5] they ensured your bum made it into the right seat and your luggage made it onto the right roof-rack.

In my experience, put an African behind the wheel of a vehicle, and he thinks the road is a speedway and the challenge is to beat it. Our driver was not just after the course honours—he was going for the world land-speed record and even some of the locals on board were stiff with fear. The whole journey became a blur of bananas and mumbled prayer. I must have blinked when we crossed the Equator, for I missed the landmark crossing completely.

Kasese, gateway to the Ruwenzori Mountains, was a low-rise, low-profile town of seemingly little importance or attraction. The nearby copper mines which buoyed the economy of Kasese, indeed Uganda itself, during the 1970s had long since closed, and with Saturday trading minimal, the town had a sort of mid-west movie-set, pre-shoot-out look about it. Save for the most enormous storks I have ever seen in my life—almost up to my shoulder in height—scavenging in the squalid entrails of forgotten kerbside dumpsters, the streets were empty.

We checked into the Saad Hotel, then mosied on down the main street to find Chris some cigarettes. A huge sign, proudly

---

[5] 100 shilling notes. At the time the rate of exchange was approximately 800 Ugandan shillings to the Australian dollar.

sponsored by Coca-Cola and unfurled above the awnings of three buildings in Margherita Road, welcomed Pope John Paul II to Kasese. For some reason he'd chosen to include the little township on his 1992 Papal Tour. The woman who eventually sold Chris his fags actually wore a souvenir teatowel commemorating the visit as a scarf, keeping—as she said—the Pontiff's image quite literally at the forefront of her mind.

Several posters sticky-taped to telegraph poles advertised additional forthcoming evangelical events, and a once-only performance by the Fort Portal Players—Uganda's premier theatrical society—was scheduled for Sunday. We enquired about tickets for the latter at the Moonlight Cafe, then heeding the proprietor's advice, lobbed down to the local police station to complete 'foreign registration' procedures. For yet more unexplainable reasons, it was mandatory for all unnative visitors to record their arrival and anticipated length of stay in Kasese, and declare all currency and objects of value in their possession. I thumbed through the ledger looking for the obvious ecclesiastical entry, but it seemed successors of St Peter were duly exempt.

Next on the afternoon agenda was a visit to the RMS—the Ruwenzori Mountaineering Services office. A large chart behind the director's desk showed a steady increase in annual visitations to the mountains, but the National Park which sanctioned them was still a relatively obscure East African destination. Compared to Kilimanjaro, which received 20 000 visitors a year, the Ruwenzori, peaking at 1102, was essentially a lost world.

There were just two short seasons a year in which it was possible to trek the Ruwenzori, the best periods being from mid-December through to the end of January and from mid-July to the end of August. It was marginally drier at those times and the bogs *en route* were reputedly thigh- (as opposed to waist-) deep.

The director of the RMS monopoly gave us a copy of the current service fees and porter rates. Most charges were up 300 per cent on the previous week, and no matter which way you looked at it, the inflated prices were not by any stretch of the imagination justifiable. If you wanted to spend more than two weeks on the trail, you needed to be—by Ugandan standards anyway—a bloody millionaire.

The RMS wanted to extort 200 000 Ugandan shillingis (Ush) for food for the porters; in reality they would spend just Ush53 000 of that amount on insufficient quantities of dried fish, cassava flour, meat, sugar and rice. The minimum amount they would charge us for fuel—which we did not intend using, having brought our own—was Ush80 000. A couple of noughts had been added to the usual 100-shillingi ticket-price for a *matatu* ride to the trail head at Ibanda. Ush20 000 was the quoted RMS fare for two.

I didn't object to paying Ush162 000 for clothing and sleeping equipment for our would-be guide and load-bearers, but when I saw the thin blankets and second-hand suit-jackets the RMS intended issuing to their commission-paying labourers, I knew I was not the only one being ripped-off. In all, our proposed 10-day trek would cost a total of Ush744 300, and the people doing all the real work would pocket collectively less than 5 per cent of that sum.

Oh, how well the Western notion of exploitation had been learned! It was one thing to make the white trash pay for the errors of their ancestors, but it was quite another to capitalise on your own flesh and blood. The RMS was sucking the life out of their black brothers, taking full advantage of the post-despot device of oppression.

Such flagrant profiteering was indicative of the corruption ethic undeveloping Africa today. But what could we do about it? Sweet F.A. Cough up, or go home.

Either way, we had to wait until Monday for the Commercial Bank to open in order to obtain the requisite funds, so we organised ourselves a little wildlife-watching adventure to fill in time on Sunday. Together with the other independent travellers lodging at the Saad, we hired a private minibus and set out on a morning tour of the Queen Elizabeth II National Park.

Shortly after sunrise our driver careered through the entrance gates, parting a sea of guinea fowl without, miraculously, scoring a single kill. A few Ugandan kob feeding at the roadside leapt out of the way, alerting the herd—concealed in the tall elephant grass behind—to our presence. The sward came alive. A thousand graceful antelopes rose as one; their sudden fright rippled through the grass like a breeze sending shock-waves through a field of sun-gold wheat. A family of wart hogs, their antenna-tails tuned to the frequency of hooves, snorted and bolted in a pig-pen cloud of confusion and dust.

To an uneducated eye, such as my own, the park was just teeming with fauna. I couldn't begin to imagine what it must have been like in its heyday.

At one time Uganda's wildlife parks were counted among the best in Africa. The QE2 once held the largest wildlife biomass in the world, but its heavyweight animals had been despoiled for fun and profit in the madness of the post-Amin era.

The northern white rhino had been annihilated, its black cousin reduced to an endangered population of six. Tens of thousands of elephants had been killed. At the time, a large ivory tusk was worth about $1000 wholesale and African rhino horn, used to make any and everything from Yemeni dagger handles to pharmaceuticals, was retailing at $15 000 a kilo in Manila and Singapore. Cheap automatic firearms—ideal weapons for poaching—were readily available in Uganda, and an alarming number of unscrupulous militants and desperate civilians sought to supplement their otherwise meagre incomes with them.

We were lucky, apparently, to see any elephants at all—let alone a herd of 35 lumbering towards the shores of Lake Rutanzige. There were only 1600 of the species left in the country, just 5 per cent of the estimated pre-civil war population.

The hippos had fared well by comparison, and the Kazinga

Channel in Queen Elizabeth II National Park was a favoured habitat. We took a boat ride down the waterway and disturbed the privacy of several thousand bellowing, wallowing, yawning half-submerged hippopotami. A myriad of water fowl and birdlife preened and fished from the banks and hundreds of water buffalo lurked in the trees behind them.

The dab safari hands on board were suitably impressed. Chris and I were totally blown away. Life in the Kazinga Channel was better than Disneyland. We returned to Kasese abuzz.

Monday morning came, and with it our pre-Ruwenzori trip to the bank. It took several hours to exchange our traveller's cheques, but alas, the wheelbarrow we anticipated using to carry away their cash equivalent remained on standby. After all, 744 300 shillingis' worth of the anticipated 50-shillingi denomination notes would have made quite a picture, but the bank manager decided such a sizeable withdrawal warranted the ceremonious unsealing of a pallet of brand-new crispy pink 1000 shillingi notes. An airline bag sufficed for their removal from his office.

We trundled off to pay the RMS their ransom and then nestled down between piles of stinking dried fish and cassava in the open tray of a battered company ute. I should have known the seats up front were too much to expect, for the cabin was clearly the *sanctum sanctorum* of freeloaders. I guess the RMS figured if we were dumb enough to have forked out 10 000 shillingis apiece for the ride, we'd be numb enough not to feel the 100-km per hour resistance of the air or notice the choking wake of passing vehicles *en route*.

We reached the village of Ibanda, at the foot of the mist-covered mountains, just after noon. Banana tree plantations covered the lower slopes of the hills all the way up to the cloud-base. Beneath it, I imagined, lay the rainforest. The air was thick with the smell of rain-drenched earth and grass, and I couldn't seem to get enough of it into my fume-and-bulldust laden lungs.

A diminutive chap named Augustine emerged from a weather-board row of offices inside the compound in which we had parked. He introduced himself as the Tourism Officer, and graciously put his subordinates at our disposal. Whatever we wished, he would command.

In spite of the regulated roster system the RMS had established to ensure equal distribution of jobs among the ever-growing fraternity of mountain guides, Augustine agreed to meet our request for the best available escort. We had a few names of people recommended by other climbers who had visited the Ruwenzoris, but hoped to hire the most experienced—Aloysius Matte.

Aloysius had actually trained all the other climbing guides. He 'knew the ropes', literally and figuratively, and was sure we'd make it to the top of the highest Ruwenzori peaks without mishap. He won me over instantly with his gentle smile and composure.

The weather appeared to be deteriorating by the minute, so Chris and I decided to forgo the customary afternoon start. We checked in to the RMS lodgings and spent the rest of the day chatting to Augustine and filming around Ibanda. That night it rained so hard Chris and I could not hear each other over the din, even when we yelled directly into one another's ears. It was as if a dam had burst, directly above the tin roof of our room.

The following morning dawned clear. At least a hundred men in gumboots had gathered outside the RMS compound, anxious to be selected as porters for our trek. As soon as Aloysius appeared at 8am they all started shouting and imploring, lest they be overlooked. Pick me! Pick me! My children have not eaten for days! I haven't worked for months! My wife is ill! I have another baby on the way! It was theatre for theatre's sake, for true to African form, Aloysius ignored the pleas and selected his team on the basis of family tie. No one objected; it was the expected outcome from the start. To give a job to a brother or fellow tribesman in Africa was not nepotism—it was an obligation.

With a great deal of scrutiny and argument the loads were sorted and weighed, resorted and weighed again, until at last the porters agreed the distribution was fair. Using fibre from the trunk of a nearby banana tree, the chosen bearers made themselves ropes and straps to suspend and balance their loads from their foreheads. The pathetic blankets we'd bought them served to pad their spines and soak up sweat; it was better to sleep with a damp rug than have one's perspiration seep through the sacking and spoil the cassava or reconstitute the fish.

Augustine issued a measure of plastic to each man to use 'in the event of rain', but assured Chris and I the 'dry' had begun in earnest and fair weather would bless us for the duration of our journey. It was not divine assurance which moved him to make such a statement, just good old tongue-in-cheek humour.

A dry season in the Ruwenzori was of course a contradiction in terms. I knew that from all I'd previously read about the infamously wet mountains. Every account this century attested to inclement weather and extremely poor visibility, day in, day out, thwarting many an attempt to reach the main summits. Cloud was so habitual, many people joked that Henry Morton Stanley was not just the first but the first and last white man ever to see the peaks from the surrounding plains. For one brief moment in history, in May, 1888, the clouds parted and the singularly privileged Stanley glimpsed the evidence many had sought to prove the existence of Ptolemy's legendary Lunae Montes.

We did not assume for a moment that we would be worthy witnesses to a second miracle, but felt confident we'd encounter better than average conditions. If the gods saw fit to grant us as little as an hour's sunshine a day, we would consider ourselves duly favoured. Brimming with optimism, we set out under an auspicious if momentarily full sun.

The trail was heavy with the previous evening's downpour. A quagmire of black mud stretched through the newly cleared fields leading up to and beyond the National Park boundary. We squelched our way through it and entered the tropical forest of the foothills.

Everything was immediately larger than life. Mammoth tree ferns and wild banana with fronds big enough to live under. Vines as thick as tree-trunks hung from emergents whose canopies were lost to the hulking evergreens of the understorey. Massive pink earthworms, as broad and brainless—indeed almost as long—as our climbing ropes, writhed in the muck underfoot.

At every turn, malicious nettles and ants with pit bull pincers were poised to prey on unwarily exposed flesh. Yet more creeping, biting and stinging things taunted from above. Their deafening cacophony of screaming and shrilling and trilling pealed over the thunderous roar of rivers, as persistent as a security alarm siren.

Within minutes of entering this luxuriant world we were absolutely drenched in sweat. Chris's temples were visibly throbbing. His core temperature must have been higher than that inside a pressure cooker. The hermetic seal on my own lid was close to breaking and I swear I could see steam jetting out from my partner's ears.

We crossed over several smaller streams which nourished the Mubuku and Mahoma rivers. They, in turn, fed Lake Albert, a major reservoir of the mighty White Nile. The trail wound onward and upward, and finally broke free of the jungle at an altitude of 2500 metres. We climbed through a belt of bamboo and out onto a narrow conifer-clad ridge. The weather closed in around us and a sudden rush of cold air replaced the tropical humidity. In a matter of minutes the temperature dropped a phenomenal 20°C. We collapsed, shivering, on the rickety steps of Nyabitaba Hut, the first or last dilapidated shelter on what the RMS called their 'seven-day-circuit'.

This was to be our home for the night, a shack of corrugated iron and masonite generously decorated with graffiti and rat poo. It looked pretty drab, but it was better than nothing.

A party of clock wise circuit trekkers dashed past, wisely

bypassing the hovel. If the mud caking their waterproofs to the thigh-tide line was anything to go by, the trail ahead had been up to its abysmal best. The expressions on their faces took us for suckers and suggested they would never be able to get out of the Ruwenzori fast enough. Some even looked as miserable as the weather they bemoaned. The buoyant ones were loudly contemplating the tilapia fish they planned to devour back at the Saad Hotel, to commemorate the end of their perambulation.

Noticing our crampons and ice-axes, one well-meaning chappie shook his head and scoffed. At least three parties, ahead of us by as few as four days, had failed to nab a single summit. For several weeks apparently, the peaks had eluded all.

It was not encouraging news. Having popped a Lariam[6] the day before, I took it badly. Abetted by the thickening gruel sky, I plunged into a black hole of depression.

Fortunately Chris was not so adversely affected by the anti-malarial drug. He professed to be undaunted by the trail ahead. Yet nothing he could say or do would lift me from the depths of panophobia. I spent the next few hours lamenting our imminent defeat: even if we made it onto the glaciers, we were bound to fall from them into the nether-nether, or disappear down a bottomless crevasse. I shuddered as I recalled an avalanche that had missed me by a whisker on Everest, and convinced myself the next one—long overdue—would be sure to true its aim first. Closer to home, I even worried that Nyabitaba would collapse and bury us in our sleep.

Fortunately it did not, and with the dawning of a new day came an easing of the Lariam-induced ill effects. I was able to shed the bulk of my irrational fears and continue on without anxiety.

I wish I could have said the same for Aloysius and our five porters, but the dread which gripped them on this fine, sun-filled morning was not so easily spent. They'd got it into their heads

---

[6] A strong anti-malarial with possible side effects of increased anxiety and depression.

that the next serviceable hut *en route*—reputedly the best, given that it was the most recently built—was possessed by a four-metre spirit, European in profile, evil in intent. There was no way our superstitious Bakonjo[7] boys wanted to risk certain death by making the scheduled overnight stopover; would we please allow them to press on to the little-used, comparatively crappy rondavel at Bigo?

Not wishing to offend them, Chris and I agreed to the change in plan. Since the extra hour or so would make the day a long one, we packed up quickly and headed off the ridge straight after breakfast.

The montane forest between Nyabitaba and the spooked John Matte[8] hut was truly enchanted, and with no help whatsoever from my imagination, we found ourselves entering a stronghold for creatures from the other side. It was Middle Earth, the perfect haunt for a lanky white ghost. Tripping almost constantly over rocks and stumbling on knotted tree-roots, I repeatedly glanced back over my shoulder and up into the gnarled, twisted boughs of the huge hagenias, expecting to catch sight of an impudent sprite. I sought goblins in the shadows between the moss-covered boulders and fairies in the wispy lichen, dangling from the skeletal fingers of ancient giant heather.

The real problem at John Matte was not aberration, but ventilation. With nothing but flimsy blankets and second-hand sports coats to keep themselves warm, the porters and guides invariably burnt charcoal all night long. To keep the heat in, they sealed off the windows of the small hut built exclusively for their use next to the tourists' bungalow. The four-metre spirit thus inflicting them with bouts of nausea and shocking headache was—in our language, anyway—the deadly apparition we call carbon monoxide poisoning.

[7] Tribal name of the inhabitants of the Ugandan side of the Ruwenzori.
[8] The hut was named in honour of Aloysius's grand-uncle John—founder of the disbanded Mountain Club of Uganda, forerunner to the RMS and the organisation responsible for building the older, original huts on the route.

As we presumed, the tourists' hut on the John Matte site was a real work of art. It even had bunk-beds! I'd never seen the likes of it on any trail back home or abroad. We sighed heavily as we passed it by.

The woodlands immediately behind the cosy cabin were the best of the day. Adjacent to them was the world's thickest natural sponge, sodden with one of the globe's highest annual rainfalls. The ground actually bounced like an inner-spring mattress when you moved across it.

As we neared Bigo hut we hit the first portion of the continent's largest intractable bogland. After sinking at the first step up to our knees, we devised a slow but successful way of hopping from one sedge tussock to the next. The grassy clumps appeared to be holding the whole oozing mass together, and four out of every five bridging strides or pot-luck leaps found their teetering mark on relatively solid ground. Every fifth footfall, however, plunged straight into thick, viscous slime.

It was tiring work for the final stretch of a tough eight-hour day, but coming from the 'it's not worth doing unless you can do it the hard way' school of trekking, we were elated by the sweet smell of sheer exhaustion. We were rewarded tenfold for our efforts when the drawbridge of cloud was lowered just before sunset, and the highest contours of the mountains assumed their corporeal form. Crowned by glaciers, Margherita and her equally regal twin, Alexandra, gazed out from their castellated kingdom in the sky.

They ruled the Ruwenzori, these stately queens of ice, like two exalted matriarchs in a make-believe realm. From such a distance their throne room seemed impossibly high.

The main bog began in earnest the following day, but its bark proved worse than its bite; we had to search for a section bad enough to warrant filming! My wildest masochistic hopes and puritanical expectations were duped by the ultimate letdown: in an effort to restrict the environmentally destructive movement of tourists through the area, the National Park wardens had built a board walk over the worst section of the fennish slop. It was regrettably indiscreet but nonetheless effective, from a conservationist's point of view, and the greenie in me was justifiably impressed, even if the pedant winced.

We reached the end of the wide, open valley floor and rose above it, through a vertical continuation of the bog. With every step forward the landscape became less credible, the plant forms more outlandish and the atmosphere increasingly fantastic. We were visitors from Lilliput, lost in the Land of the Giants, Tim and Lex, alone in Jurassic Park.

Ordinary plants had grown to extraordinary sizes; gargantuan groundsels 15 metres high and colossal lobelias as tall as telegraph poles flourished in untameable abundance. Mist swirled, dissolved, reformed anew and enveloped the scene in silence. The distant mountains lay brooding beneath their interminable cloud. A chill set in to the bone.

It was totally prehistoric; a eulogy to the earth's primordial past. No wind stirred; no creature moved. The world, it seemed, was holding its breath. It was as it always had been, since the dawn of time.

Further on and higher still, Bujuku Lake floated in a kohl-lined orbit. Slate grey and motionless, staring without blinking at the sky, it was surely the eye of a great resting cyclops. We tiptoed past, clinging to the brow of stone, afraid to even whisper, should we break the spell which kept the mythical beast in slumber.

Something or someone from every fairytale ever told had found its way into this strange, eerie land. It was Grimm, it was Tolkien, it was Spielberg; it was a world all three masters of the far-fetched and fantastic had conspired, across time, to create.

We reached the campsite of Bujuku, nestled at the foot of Stuhlman Pass, just on 3pm. It was day three on the trail, and miraculously, it still hadn't rained. Heaven forbid, the sun was even shining! Right on cue the clouds curtaining the peaks opened and

GOD HELP ME
PASS 2318

En Route to Malealea,
Lesotho.

Sorrel with
Malehlohono Lo
Monyane in Malealea
village, Lesotho.

Ha Nohana village, Lesotho.

The view from Sani Pass looking down into South Africa.

Morning smoke fills the valleys of the Drakensberg - viewed from Menoaneng Pass, Lesotho.

David approaching the Thaba Putsoa Range, Lesotho.

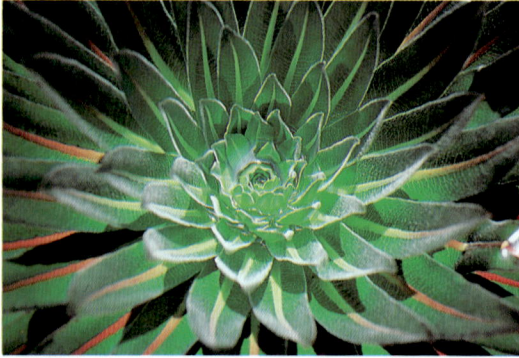

Close up of a young lobelia plant, Ruwenzori Mountains, Uganda.

Moss and groundsel on Freshfield Pass, Ruwenzori Mountains, Uganda.

Chris and Alosius Matte, approaching the final route to the summit of Margherita on Mount Stanley, Ruwenzoris, Uganda.

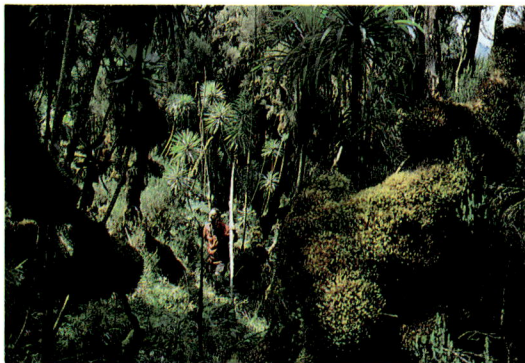

Chris in the forest near John Matte Hut on the Ruwenzori trail, Uganda.

Chris bogged down in the Ruwenzoris, Uganda.

Memie, Loita Hills, Kenya.

Robert Oloimooja ole Rerente. Loita Plains

Kokoo, one of Robert's four 'mothers' in Narotian village, Loita Hills, Kenya.

Meiyoki's enkaiyoni,
Loita Hills, Kenya.

Catherine and
Robert's daughter,
Ndoondo.
Loita Hills, Kenya.

The vast Rift Valley
floor on the evening of
our last night-trek
with the Maasai.

The sulphuric world of Ol Doinyo Le Enkai crater.

Jewellery and carved bone, Kenyan markets.

we were audience to a most unexpected and marvellous matinee. The sinister, hunchbacked dome of Mount Baker loomed centre-stage, the crowned peaks of Mount Stanley reappeared in the right gallery and hidden behind the rocky wing directly on the left, sat the formidable massif of Mount Speke.

That night the drama unfolding in the natural amphitheatre was enhanced by a myriad of stars. The earth shook with one of its frequent tremors and, contemplating the universe for the ump-teenth time, I knew we were destined to succeed.

Clear skies continued well into the next day, cheering us on as Aloysius led the way up the side of our first chosen summit. Vit-torio Emanuele, at 4890 metres, was the highest point on Speke and we reached it just seconds before the anticipated clouds. We didn't even have time to pose for the obligatory mountaintop photo. We were in the midst of a white-out; our visibility was reduced to zero.

In spite of the untimely weather change, we couldn't have been more excited. Aloysius confided the peak posed a greater climbing challenge than Margherita on neighbouring Mount Stanley, and as far as he was concerned we had nothing to worry about at all. The highest prize of the Ruwenzori was well within our reach. If Kitasamba,[9] the presiding deity, continued to ride within gunshot, we were pretty well home and hosed.

It was the greatest confidence-booster, the ultimate reassurance. Chris was now adept at cramponing, and by roping together, the last of my worries faded. If any of us fell, the only thing we'd lose now was our pride.

We retraced our steps off the summit, crossed the Speke Glacier, abseiled and front-pointed down its snout and bouldered back to safety.

On returning to the Bujuku hut we were cold, thirsty and totally buggered, but nonetheless beaming. A few other trekking

[9] Kitasamba—the supreme Creator of the Universe.

parties had arrived on the scene, including one group of eleven 'overlanders',[10] stretching their legs for the first time since leaving London. Half of them were originally from New Zealand and their familiar accents and friendly greetings soon warmed us from the inside out.

It was not easy getting out of bed the next morning. Eighteen people in all, lying like sardines on the two sleeping platforms and floor, meant any sort of movement disturbed the lot. Despite the cramped quarters, Chris and I had slept well, but for some reason the old batteries had failed to recharge. Masked by exhilaration, the exertion of yesterday had taken its toll overnight. I personally felt I could sleep for a week.

We were faring a great deal better than some of our bedmates, however. One poor woman had been up all night with Ugandan-nutella[11] poisoning. A Swiss couple and two of the overlanders had altitude-related headaches and nausea. One of the New Zealanders thought he was coming down with malaria.

Of the eighteen, just two would continue on to complete the full seven-day circuit. Chris and I and one other woman named Kristen were side-trekking up to Elena hut in order to have a go at Margherita. The remaining thirteen were heading back the way they had come, because of their illnesses and itinerary constraints.

Our route for the day was a doozey. No bog, admittedly, but in its place the gods had laid a stairway straight to heaven—lining it with knee-deep mud. When that ended, there were slippery, freezing cold metal ladders to climb and the track beyond them, leading towards Omukabam-wanjara Ridge, zigzagged up a sheer slope of sliding scree and loose grey dust.

At 4540 metres the weather swirling around Elena hut was ghastly. The porters came up with the supplies we needed to survive and climb, then turned on their heels and ran back to

---

[10] People travelling overland through Africa on an extended organised vehicular tour. They usually motor from site to site in specially designed 'adventure machines', fully equipped converted trucks.
[11] Nutella is a sandwich spread made from chocolate and hazelnuts.

Bujuku. This was no place to spend the night without the best possible sleeping bag and layer upon layer of warm clothing. Fortunately Aloysius had hired an adequate bag from the RMS, as had Kristen's guide, Matthew. Previous climbers had bequeathed a variety of jackets, pullovers and thick socks to their cause, so the pair weren't too badly dressed for the occasion, either. Aloysius, thanks to one of our proud sponsors, even had a brand new pair of lightweight leather climbing boots. Matthew, adhering to Ruwenzori fashion, intended to strap the necessary crampons directly to his gumboots.

The five of us wasted no time getting into our sleeping bags and quickly primed the stoves for tea. Elena was one of the few huts in the Ruwenzori where climbers and their 'staff' were not segregated, so at last we had the chance to enlarge our experience of the mountains by getting to know more about those who lived and worked within them.

It was a pity other tourists didn't have such opportunities to share more than trail-time with their guides. It wasn't always easy to talk and walk at the same time, so few people left the Ruwenzori with little more than a feeling for their loyal chaperon. Since the porters moved as a team from point A to point B without stopping, many tourists would not even come to know their names, or be able to recognise them in a crowd.

This was something that always saddened me. Here, it was the fault of the system as much as it was of the individual and reinforced the cruellest of colonialism's divisive legacies: the lingering inferiority complex. True, we were paying these guys to do a job for us and even in the West that scenario created a certain—if artificial—'them and us' set-up. But in the West, such relationships were well defined and everyone—regardless of their position—maintained a clear sense of identity. Here, I couldn't help but feel that that had been confused.

Many die-hard old-school expeditioners would argue that division was the key to keeping 'the show on the road', as it were.

Once you start treating the troops as equals, you lose their respect. The best you could hope for was a mutiny.

Well ... we'd seen plenty of those during our time in the Himalaya, but most occurred not because of any real attempt by either side to see eye-to-eye—they were invariably the result of a total lack of understanding, a failure to bridge through genuine empathy and friendship, the cultural and economic gulf created by personal circumstances and the consequences of history.

In perpetuating the colonial approach, the RMS was denying Bakonjos and tourists alike the chance to effect a change; not to right past wrongs, but to actually start something new. If all tourism meant to the RMS was dollars, then ultimately they, and everyone in their employ, would be poorer for the experience as well.

Chris, Kristen and I were grateful for this long-awaited opportunity to exchange views, not simply look at them. There was so much more to the Ruwenzori than mud and mountains, so much more to Uganda than Amin and AIDS. There was also a lot more besides our comparative wealth to share with Aloysius and Matthew.

Our common ground was, of course, our common enemy: the RMS. But in discussing the organisation, we came to learn a great deal about the lot of our porters and guides and their political attitudes, as well as their families, their spiritual and theological beliefs—the day-to-day realities of their lives.

In the course of our conversation, I asked Matthew (who, as it transpired, was Aloysius's younger brother) if the Ruwenzori was home to a Big-foot or Yeti-like creature. It was something that had crossed my mind more than once on the trek so far. Given the nature of the terrain and the ambience or mood it invoked, I would have been surprised if the superstitious Bakonjo had no such legend.

Matthew looked at me, his eyes widening. He looked across to Aloysius for help. Yes, they had such a beast, but to mention its name was to call it forth from its hiding place. They debated whether or not writing its name in my notebook would have the same effect, and realising that that was how they themselves had been told of the huge gorrilla-like, low-grunting, man-eating beast, they pencilled the name in my diary. I thanked them, and swore never to repeat it publicly.

As we all talked, we roasted and ate our way through the bulk of a two-kilogram bag of peanuts. There was nothing wrong with our appetites at altitude, but enough was enough; we were starting to feel sick from the indulgence. We decided to use what remained as an offering to our respective gods and old what's-his-name, the Yeti.

Hamming it up, Kristen and I tossed peanuts in the four directions of the winds, beseeching the benevolence of Kitasamba, Buddha, Jesus Christ and half-a-dozen other internationally renowned celestial deities. Matthew and Aloysius joined in, laughing and giggling at the cheek of it all, clearly amazed to see us doing something so utterly ridiculous. It wasn't sacrilegious; it was just *mad*! I got the distinct feeling that white-woman humour had taken the brothers completely by surprise.

When the next day dawned, the first of our peanut-prayers were answered. There was not a single cloud in the sky. As far as the eye could see there was nothing but blue. Even the valleys way below us were clear. It was simply remarkable.

Aloysius, who had climbed Margherita at least a dozen times and circuited the mountains more often than he could remember, could not recall a day as magnificent as this. We were truly blessed.

Anxious to make the most out of our good fortune, we were out of the hut by 7am, rock-hopping our way over the troughs and ridges left by a historically much larger Elena Glacier. At the turn of the century the giant tongue of ice protruding from the lip of Stanley Plateau extended well below the contemporary location of the hut, but it was now a good half-hour above it.

Continuing glacial retreat was a natural process, but recent acceleration in global warming—commonly called the 'greenhouse effect'—had already robbed the Ruwenzori of its lesser glaciers and was forcing the bigger ones to recede at the alarming average rate of eight metres a year. Once they were gone, the face of these legendary Mountains of the Moon would change forever. The lives of the Bakonjo—indeed the existence of just about everyone living below the watershed, even those over six and a half thousand kilometres away at the other end of the mighty Nile—would surely be affected.

It was a hell of a thing to be contemplating, as we strapped on our crampons, slapped on the sun screen, roped up and dug the blades of our ice-axes into Elena's 'snout'. I felt a bit guilty frontpointing into the ice; it was a bit like kicking a dog when it was already down.

We were on the Stanley Plateau by 8am. Margherita and Alexandra stood directly in front of us at the far side of the kilometre-wide plain of snow, resplendent under the full equatorial sun. We could see right across the entire range, ridge on ridge, blue on blue.

Immediately to our left was Mount Moebius, an isolated pinnacle of rock on the plateau, spectacularly corniced with rime frost. Ice fragments had accumulated on the windward-side of the peak, creating a series of fantastic hanging blooms and shrubs. It was as if Moebius, resembling an inverted volcano caught in the throes of a massive eruption, had suddenly frozen solid.

We walked beneath the mountain, beneath a billowing dream of fairy-floss and cauliflower cloud. Melting icicles of every size hung in organ-pipe clusters beneath, like lashes of light, shedding tears of pure crystal, white on white, jewel on jewel.

Never in my life had I imagined anything on earth could be as beautiful as this.

To climb to the summit of Margherita from the far side of the plateau we had to first drop down below the southeast ridge of

Alexandra, then ascend the Margherita Glacier to the col, or saddle, bridging the two queens of Mount Stanley. The weather was still favouring us, but it was anyone's guess how long it would last. The real-time speed of Ruwenzori clouds was faster than Sky-Cam on the six-thirty news.

The snowfield condition was absolutely perfect, but so much direct sunshine was quickly turning the steep face of Margherita's glacier to slush. It was hard work descending it as every thrust of the ice-axe or kick of a crampon caused the old glacier to leak like a sieve.

I'd spent a great deal of time worrying over the anticipated crevasses on the Alexandra-Margherita col, but they were nothing compared to those I'd encountered above the icefall on Everest, and very easily avoided.

The view from the saddle was incredible. We moved as close to the edge of it as we dared, and stared straight down a 1000-metre vertical shute into Zaire. A pall of smoke hung over the troubled nation, but beneath it the land was a vivid emerald green. The juxtaposed landscapes, the contrast of snow and ice and jagged ranges on one side and tropical jungle on the other, were simply breathtaking.

And so was the route Aloysius chose to take up Margherita— only horrifyingly so. He led the way onto a face of the summit pyramid that seemed to protude directly above the freefall route into Zaire.

For ten precarious minutes, alternately balanced on the front points of our crampons and the pick-ends of our ice-axes, we climbed above the void.

An electrifying current of adrenalin ran through my body. An intoxicating mix of excitement and terror swilled inside my mind. I had a lead weight in my stomach, a desert in my mouth. Courage and fear were entwined like lovers in my heart. They were its rhythm. They were its song. They were the majesty co-eternal.

We reached the top of the snowline and paused to take off our crampons. The last 50 metres of the climb was a scramble up a slope of loose rocks, and to take it safely we stayed roped up. Kristen and Matthew were waiting for us on the summit, calling and screaming and laughing and jeering us towards the finish line.

Right on cue, the inevitable clouds came from nowhere and obscured the Ruwenzori's premier vista. Four full hours of brilliant sunshine came to an abrupt end, but we were too busy hugging each other to care. The delirium of success was all-consuming.

We stayed on top of Margherita for half an hour, waiting for the view to return. When it didn't, we realised we were in danger of losing visibility as well, so we quickly launched ourselves into the descent.

Within two hours we were back at Elena, cutting it fine with the timing. The bad weather was definitely settling in—not just for the afternoon, but for good. The clouds were getting lower by the minute and before we knew it, the mist rising up from the valley below closed in around us like a shroud. It started to sleet.

Chris was grinning like a Cheshire cat regardless. He was a real climber now, and justifiably proud of it. According to the notes I was carrying, what we had just completed ranked a two on the International Grading System for technical difficulty. It was no big deal to the Messners of the world, but to novices like us it was quite an achievement. We celebrated with the last of our chocolate bars and a cuddle.

The porters arrived up from Bujuku at noon the following day. Aloysius had come down with a fever and stomach cramps during the night, so it was fortuitous the team arrived ahead of schedule. We had planned to spend the day exploring more of the area, but it had been too bitter to even go outside the hut, let alone further afield.

We didn't know what was ailing Aloysius, but agreed it would be dangerous to hang out at Elena waiting for him to improve. Altitude was debilitating even if you were healthy, so we began retreating from it as soon as the porters had readied their loads.

If descending failed to lower his temperature, at least it raised his spirits. By the time we reached Kitandara Lakes, Aloysius was smiling again. He wasn't up to climbing Mount Baker, though, even after a good night's sleep, so we passed up the last of our intended climbs and set about finishing the circuit.

Two days were all it took to get back to Ibanda—two magic days of tripping and stumbling and impaling ourselves on concealed obstacles, two days of wading through knee-deep bog, two days of mist and moss and heather and rock. The terrain never ceased to amaze us; if anything, it was even more enchanting than that we'd encountered on the route in.

We returned to the Saad Hotel in Kasese, and headed straight for the bathroom. It took hours to scrub the dirt from our clothes and to soak the mud off our boots, but no amount of rubbing or showering would take the smiles from our faces. We'd carried them all the way down from the summit of Margherita, and fully intended wearing them back to Kenya and beyond.

Ah, it felt so good to be alive!

HOME OF THE MAASAI,
LAND OF THE BRAVE

RETURNING TO KENYA was a sobering experience. The express coach that carried us to Kampala left half an hour late from Kasese, which, by chance, saved us from a fate worse than death. Somewhere between the townships of Bushenyi and Mbarara, we came across a scene we could so easily have been a part of—had our driver chosen to leave on time. Soldiers who had retained their guns, but not their stripes, in the government's recent culling of the troops, had just waylaid, shot up and looted a bus and a *matatu*. Several people had been killed and many injured.

The vehicles were abandoned in the middle of the road; glass, blood and bananas littered the highway. Passengers who'd escaped into nearby fields had not yet returned to sift through their ransacked belongings, but the dead and wounded had been taken by other passing vehicles to Mbarara Hospital. The police were yet to put in an appearance.

Maasailand

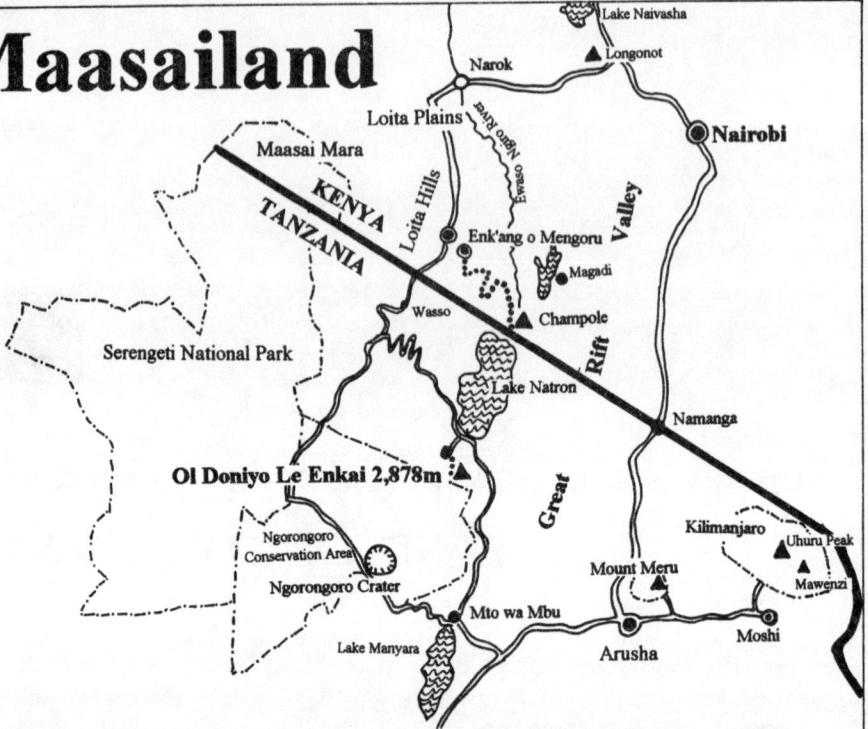

Lake Naivasha
Narok
Longonot
Loita Plains
Nairobi
Maasai Mara
KENYA
TANZANIA
Loita Hills
Ewaso Ngiro River
Enk'ang o Mengoru
Rift
Valley
Magadi
Wasso
Champole
Serengeti National Park
Lake Natron
Namanga
Ol Doniyo Le Enkai 2,878m
Great
Ngorongoro
Conservation Area
Kilimanjaro
Uhuru Peak
Ngorongoro Crater
Mount Meru
Mawenzi
Mto wa Mbu
Lake Manyara
Arusha
Moshi

UGANDA KENYA
ZAIRE
Ol Doniyo
Le Enkai
Loita Hills
TANZANIA
MOZAMBIQUE

We stopped briefly to permit the curious and ghoulish a closer look at the wreckage, then continued on our way as if nothing much had happened. Our fellow travellers were roused by the experience for a moment or two, but after that, they just went back to sleep on each other's shoulders. It was obviously no big deal in a country where atrocities had long been par for the course. It would be a long time indeed before the guerillas in their midst made it onto an endangered species list.

Ambush was the crime flavour of the month in Kenya as well, and on returning to Nairobi, it seemed as if every expatriate had a first- or second-hand story about a car theft at gunpoint to tell us. Unwary tourists were a particularly favoured target, and at least a dozen dream safaris had come to an abrupt end recently on some isolated stretch of road between Nairobi and the great Rift Valley or Mombasa. Several foreign residents had been forced from their vehicles on the Langatta Road, and one had been killed the minute he refused. New 4WDs were going missing from Kenyatta Airport's parking lot and one diplomat was shot dead for his, right out in front of the city museum, in broad daylight.

Burglaries were ever-popular, and every well-to-do household in the capital had electrified or reinforced fences, sophisticated alarm systems, an around-the-clock tag-team of *askaris*[1] and regular surveillance services. In spite of all that, most homes were still subjected to at least one attempted robbery per year. We just so happened to be staying with Paul Cameron, the technical officer from the Australian High Commission, and his wife Susan, the night their turn came around.

The police were pretty useless in controlling crime waves or catching criminals. Nine times out of ten they weren't even capable of showing up when called to a crime scene. Susan told us how once, when she was living alone, she had telephoned her local police office to report a burglary in action—only to be asked

[1] Watchmen or guards.

if she would mind driving down to the station to fetch the police assistance she required, as all the force vehicles were out of petrol and thus inoperable.

Fortunately for us, Paul's house was protected by one of several private security companies which were operating in the somewhat salubrious area. They were on the scene within minutes. It was imperative to quiz even them, however, as several gangs were currently posing as roaming safeguard squads, conning their way onto properties, then pillaging them for all they were worth.

These were desperate times, not just in Kenya, but right across the continent. Never had the gap between the First and Third Worlds seemed so wide. Journalists had started referring to Africa as the Nth World, so blighted, so bereft, they couldn't even put a figure on it.

There seemed no end to the human tragedy of Africa. The statistics were impossible to digest. There were officially ten million refugees[2] and 181 million unemployed adults scattered across the continent. Some 220 million Africans—almost half of the population south of the Sahara—lived in absolute poverty, unable to meet their most basic needs. Eighty million children under the age of five were chronically malnourished and nearly two million of them died every year from diarrhoeal diseases—a figure equivalent to the entire population of Brisbane perishing year after year, generation after generation.

The statistics were so mind-boggling they had little or no effect when you heard them on the news or read them in a book. It was only when you drove past a refugee camp—like the one which sprawled along the Mathare Valley just north of Nairobi—or visited a public (as opposed to private) hospital in the city, that the misery they manifested really hit home. The day I saw a petrol-sniffing six-year-old, blood and mucus gushing like a river from his nose, screaming as he fought for his life on a crowded

[2] This figure is constantly in flux. The following year another two million displaced persons, mostly from Burundi and Rwanda, substantially bolstered the continent's refugee ranks.

street of Nairobi's CBD, was one of the most distressing and pathetic I can ever remember in my life. He was so young, so small, so vulnerable. He was being pulverised by his homeless peers for the 10 lousy shillingis he'd just begged to feed not himself, but his dependency. I don't know how many weeks—dare I even suggest years—he had left to live, but his eyes and his heart had been dead forever.

It made little difference whether we were in South Africa, Uganda, Kenya or any one of a score or so of sub-Saharan countries—the health, wealth and welfare situation was hopeless. Kenya was a lot better off than many others, ranking 25 out of the 124 countries registered in the World Development Report. Its problems were nowhere near as bad as those facing neighbouring Tanzania, Ethiopia and Somalia—the second, third and fourth poorest nations in the world respectively—so at least we were able to chew on the statistics concerning our new East African 'home', bitter though they were.

Kenya was considered to be the capitalist model of black Africa, even though 50 per cent of the over-15 population were unemployed. I'm quite sure there were more beggars on the streets of Nairobi than there were in New Delhi: whole families camped outside banks, children worked the traffic intersections, even retrenched businessmen wearing suits and expressions of total humiliation solicited for handouts. There was no such thing as the dole here, and coming from a society which allocated nearly 40 per cent of its national budget expenditure to social security and welfare, I found the abject poverty engendered in the glitzy, glassy, First World-looking CBD of Nairobi totally incomprehensible.

The 3.9 per cent per annum population growth was fast turning the city into chaos. Waves of people were washing in from the land every day, looking for an answer to their rural woes—but they would find no shelter here, and even fewer job opportunities.

On the health front, Kenya's records painted an equally bleak picture. There was roughly one doctor per 7500 people and one hospital bed for every 734 potential patients. Australia's statistics, by comparison, were one to 438, and one to 199 respectively.[3] The nation lay smack bang in the middle of the world's 'meningitis belt' and tuberculosis was widespread in the greater rural community. Other fatal and debilitating endemic diseases included malaria, bilharzia, yellow fever, dengue fever, and sleeping sickness.

All things considered, it was downright bizarre to find one of the most popular guidebooks for travellers on the market intimating that Kenya was not unlike Switzerland: among the safest and healthiest countries in the world! While admitting that violent crime did exist, the guide just dismissed the issue as inconsequential, since it 'seldom involved tourists'. Obviously, as visitors, we were meant to restrict our movements to the game park/hotel circuit and concern ourselves only with the trivial experiences indicative of the vapid 'sightseeing' style of tourism this and other books of its genre promoted.

I am no alarmist; nor do I go out of my way to track down facts and figures for the purpose of nourishing some peculiar neurosis. I sought out—and now repeat—such information in order to keep a valid perspective on the big African picture. It was so easy, otherwise, for someone like me to get swept away by the romance and write of nothing else. It was, after all, what I assumed most people wanted to hear.

The lot of Kenya's people, whatever their race, was rarely deemed of interest. The plight of the rhino was far more important to the international audience, and seeing one in the wild was what Africa was really all about. The quintessential experience here was sighting the 'Big Five' in a single day of touring: rhino, lion, leopard, elephant and buffalo. Who cared about the Maasai, upon whose land this wildlife roamed?

Because of the general preoccupation with four-legged

[3] All statistics are taken from the *Encyclopaedia Brittanica* 1993 yearbook.

creatures, and the infrastructure needed to satisfy it, there were few genuine opportunities for tourists with a more human focus to enjoy anything beyond the most contrived encounter with the Maasai, many of whom stationed themselves like inanimate attractions at key points along the game-drive routes where for anything from one to 500 shillingis, they would allow you to take the stereotypical photograph they presumed you sought.

At the entrances to some game reserves, replicated Maasai villages or *enk'angs* have been established for a less superficial—but equally artificial and commercial—contact. A quick welcome song and dance, followed by a frenzied sale of artefacts, was hardly what I'd call a meaningful cultural exchange, but it was the best most tourists could hope for.

It was hardly surprising that most people left Kenya with absolutely no understanding of or empathy with the Maasai. They were the race who had always been the foremost human face of Africa, the continent's bi-ped lions. But here, centre stage, where most of the world would meet them for the very first and perhaps only time, they were merely props, stripped of their mystique and robbed of their pride, their value reduced to the price of a postcard.

Chris and I had a unique chance to experience a truer cameo of Maasai life in the Kenyan Loita Hills. I had known Catherine Oddie—the Australian girl whose wedding to Maasai warrior Robert Oloimooja ole Rerente featured on a special *60 Minutes* program—for many years, and in the course of researching our expedition had re-established contact with her. We had grown up in the same street and gone to the same schools, and when I did my stint as a regular guest on the *Bert Newton Show* in late 1989, our paths had crossed again. She was working for the agency I'd chosen to handle my contract, and we spoke regularly over the phone.

At that time, I remember Catherine telling me she was heading off to Africa to photograph zebras. Falling in love with a lithe, pastoral Maasai was not exactly what she had planned along the way. In fact, marriage was probably the furthest thing from her mind.

Robert's subsequent visit to Australia coincided with the planning phase of our African expedition. *60 Minutes* had paid for him and a friend to fly out from Kenya in order to facilitate filming the 'sequel' to his very public union with Catherine. The newlyweds came down to Ulladulla for a few days between shoots, which gave Chris an opportunity to meet Catherine and both of us the chance to get aquainted with Robert.

My brother-in-law and two of his kids were staying with us at the time, and as usual a constant stream of friends passed through our humble doors. Robert's stories kept everyone enthralled: how he came to acquire each scar on his sleek and hairless legs, and how his spear was the one to pierce the lion hunted down by his age-group during the second phase of their warriorhood. Catherine's tales were equally fascinating, but my just-teenage niece had great difficulty coming to terms with the way she so willingly accepted Robert's taking of a second wife. The very idea appalled her, and she could ask Catherine about little else.

Catherine had always been a bright and bubbly lady, but temporarily seemed to be suffering from a case of media-induced cynicism. Her experience with the first *60 Minutes* episode was largely to blame. She was very bitter about it, and unfortunately she had committed herself and her husband to a follow-up story before the first had even gone to air.

When we met with Catherine again in Nairobi on our return from Uganda she seemed pretty stressed. She was the first to admit she had 'torn a hole in her universe' which she would never be able to repair. Selling her story to the media had been the biggest mistake of her life, and she worried that Robert's family would no longer accept her.

She had been looking forward to her delayed homecoming for ages. Having opted to stay on alone in Australia after the second story, in order to work and save some money, she had been away for a little over eight months. In her absence, Robert's 'friend'—the one who had travelled with him for the *60 Minutes* follow-up—had done his damnedest to discredit Catherine, and now her dreams of returning to her husband's village were plagued with uncertainty.

Motivated primarily by jealousy, the 'friend' had apparently spread a number of vicious rumours and shown certain members of the clan the initial *60 Minutes* tape. Selective editing and a couple of very off-the-cuff 'Aussie' remarks Catherine had made during the interview sequences had, to some extent, misrepresented the Maasai, and according to recent conversations Catherine had had with Robert by phone, some of the people in the Loitas were far from impressed. She hoped with all her heart that her immediate family would be a little more understanding and see the situation for what it was, but until she reached their *enk'ang*, she didn't know how she would be received.

We travelled up to the Loitas together, Catherine, Chris and I, early in August. The 4WD we'd hired between us was loaded to the hilt with everything from presents for Ndoondo—the daughter gifted to Catherine by Robert's brother shortly after she and 'Bob' were married—and bales of hay and newspaper to start a permaculture garden.

It took the whole day to drive to the village of Narotian from Nairobi, across the floor of the Great Rift Valley and beyond to the sacred hill country of the Laibon, the spiritual leaders of the Maasai people. The sheer beauty of the landscape lifted Catherine from her reverie and distracted her thoughts from her family.

For Chris and me, looking down on the rift from the edge of its dramatic, sweeping wall for the first time was simply marvellous. If Kilimanjaro was the rooftop of Africa, then here was the continent's basement: a massive fault in the earth's surface, visible even from the moon. We glimpsed just a fragment of the 8700-km long system of cracks which ran from the Jordan Valley in the Middle East to the Zambezi Delta in Mozambique, rending the earth's crust like an opening zipper.

The rift was nowhere more sharply defined than here, cutting as it did through the Kenyan highlands. The mean drop for the whole rift was between 600 and 900 metres, but in parts of Kenya it averaged as much as 2700 metres. From the lofty escarpment near Limuru on the road from Nairobi to Lake Naivasha, it was incredible to see just how far the valley floor had settled from its original elevation. The other side of the slowly sinking vale was too far away to see, but we guessed from our maps that this section of the vast crack in the African plate was some 50 kilometres wide.

Right in the middle of this portion of the Great Rift Valley sat the extinct volcanic cones of Longonot and Suswa. In the early morning light they had an almost mystical look; indeed, they completely compelled our attention as we drove directly towards then past them.

We did not expect to see wildlife *en route* to Narotian. Assuming that animals were somehow confined to the designated game parks and reserves in the country, our drive across the Great Rift was all the better for our lack of anticipation. We were like two kindy-kids on a first excursion to the zoo, playing spot the giraffe and count the gazelle.

It was very dry on the Loita Plain, below the hills, but every now and then the monotony of the listless, barren scape was broken by a movement—a zebra, a mongoose, an ostrich. Occasionally a junior warrior wearing an exotic headdress of tiny dead birds came into view, or a red-robed, spear-carrying herdsman emerged with his cattle from the distant shimmering heat like a vision in a dream.

I felt my heart skip a beat every time a warrior appeared on the horizon or between the static thorn trees. In spite of everything Catherine had told me, I doubted the Maasai were able to hold to their traditional ways, under a government that was actively doing all it could to subdue or wipe their culture out. But here they were, so far from the city; so removed from the process of progress, defiant and proud, living up to everything they stood for.

The threat of drought was always imminent; it had been a part of Maasai life for endless centuries. Their culture was somehow fortified by it; their spirits strengthened, not defeated. But official discrimination and suspect political policy were unfamiliar forces entirely, and whether the Maasai as a nation would be able to resist and survive them was uncertain. They had been delivered an ultimatum, not a choice: cooperate with the future, or be engulfed by it.

Potentially, the worst destructions would be wrought by the government schemes, currently gaining ground, to privatise all Maasai land. If they were implemented, all previous community-owned territory would be parcelled and title given to individual men, most of whom had no idea of the ramifications of such a system. Within only a few years, having been tempted to sell for short-term gain, many Maasai would surely find themselves legally landless. They'd be turfed off their own pastures and forced to migrate into the city or shantytowns, or work as hired hands for the rich developers who would inevitably buy up a swag of individual plots. The lifestyle of the Maasai, not to mention their whole culture, would change irrevocably.

Those sensitive to the cause of the Maasai were suggesting this development was worse than anything the pastoralists had recently confronted. It was a contemporary crisis, on a par with the theft of their best pasture lands during the colonial era. They faced a desperate struggle against civilisation which would surely threaten them with the same desolate fate of the North American Indians.

We reached Narotian just after 3pm. The stubble of grass around Catherine and Robert's home was tawny and brittle, the yellow-barked fever trees brazen and tall. We pulled up in a cloud of dust alongside their dung-daubed hut, stretching as we climbed out of the cramped quarters of the vehicle. The peaceful soul of the place was almost palpable.

One by one the women of the family compound came to greet Catherine. She need not have worried—their excitement at her return was obvious. They hugged and kissed her, laughing and smiling with genuine warmth. We were introduced, but it was really Catherine's moment, so we left her to it and started unloading the car.

Ndoondo was still at infants' school, but expected home any minute. Robert was away, imparting his knowledge of the region and teaching associated bushcraft skills to a bunch of American students attending Kenya's National Outdoor Leadership School. When he returned, he and his brothers planned to take Chris and me trekking. He was expected back in a couple of days and in the meantime we had promised to help Catherine get a few things done around her home in the enk'ang.

Her thatched-roof house was pretty small, just one square room, divided into sections by woven partitions. The first, broken by the doorway, sort of formed a narrow passageway running parallel to the front of the hut. It was used primarily for storage, but in the corner just behind the door there were a small table and a basin held in a canvas sling, which constituted the bathroom. Behind that, screened by the left-hand side of the interior 'wall' was a traditional bed, a large hide stretched taut on a wooden frame. Crammed into the chamber on the right was a big Western-style double bed. The middle area between served as the kitchen, lounge room, reception hall and office. It was less than three metres square.

There were few amenities, if any—no electricity, no running water, no gas stove, no toilet, no shower. Catherine, like her Maasai sisters in-law, had to squat in the scrub, fetch her water from a mere trickle of a stream several hundred metres away, wash in a basin, prepare food and read by candlelight and cook on an open fire.

To make life a little easier, she'd brought a few gadgets with her from Australia; a solar-panel to power a battery which would charge a small fluoro light and laptop computer, a doona, a few kitchen knives and a potato peeler. She was not yet adept at chopping wood, so she paid one of her relatives to do it for her. The forest where they collected dead timber was quite a way from the *enk'ang*, and fetching enough for a week usually took half a day.

Catherine paid quite a few people to do odd jobs for her, actually, a practice well suited to the changing needs of the community. With a little extra cash, the women were able to buy small things like beads to make jewellery to sell and wear, or sugar to sweeten their tea. In the new economic order they needed money for school fees, uniforms and books for their children. Catherine, on the other hand, needed time—to spend writing her book about life with her Maasai family—so the arrangement worked in everyone's favour.

Catherine had done everything she could to avoid being seen as a one-woman aid organisation, but history conspired against her. The only other whites who had ever settled in the area were missionaries. They meant well, but many Maasai had come to take their handouts for granted.

Catherine had strict rules about 'visiting hours', but was nearly always too soft-hearted to enforce them. Over the next few days, as she endeavoured to get her house and new garden in order, women, children and *moran*[4] came and went from her home in a never-ending parade—borrowing this, cadging that, or waiting for her to stop what she was doing so she could serve them milky tea.

It must have been enormously difficult to come from a society such as ours into this *mélange*, and I really admired the way

---

[4] Warriors.

Catherine coped—on her terms. It took a lot of guts.

While Chris and I pitched our tent in the 'front yard', we tried to come to grips with the complicated set up of Robert's family. His father, who had passed away 18 months beforehand, had taken four wives. On our way to the Loitas, Catherine had referred to them all as 'Robert's mothers', but his real birth mum—who lived in another compound with Robert's other wife several hours walk away in Morijo—was the one she said she called Mama. Of the father's other wives, two lived in Narotian and their names were Kokoo and Mumai. Both of the matriarchs wandered over to see what we were up to, and welcome us—as friends of Catherine's—to their compound.

Mumai was very old, with the sad look of a bloodhound about her, but Kokoo was as vibrant as a rainbow, ageless and magnificent. Mumai lived with one of her sons, his wife and their three children in a loaf-shaped, soot-blackened dwelling at the far end of the five-hut *enk'ang*. Kokoo lived alone, but as we were soon to realise, she had no time to feel lonely. She was constantly receiving and entertaining people at her hearth.

Robert had four full-brothers, three full-sisters, two half-brothers, one adopted brother, three half-sisters, 16 brothers and sisters-in-law, 40 nephews, nieces, half-nephews and half-nieces and who knew how many cousins—half, quarter or otherwise. Regardless of the actual strength or weakness of a bloodline, all family members were treated equally, and Catherine pointed out that Robert made no distinctions whatsoever in defining his siblings and in-laws; he spoke of them all in the generic Maasai terms for full brother and sister.

Just to confuse the issue a tad further, Catherine explained that relatives—and indeed friends—were not necessarily referred to by name *or* relationship; in adherence to an unusual tradition, they were called by the name of the gift given to consolidate or establish particular social bonds with one another. Thus one of Robert's nephews, whose real name was Loldudula, was called

Pa-ashe by Catherine, since he had given her a calf for a wedding present. Similarly, Robert and his full-brother James reciprocally addressed each other as 'Pa-kiteng'—from the Maasai word for cow—since, in accordance to custom, they had given each other an adult milker.

Robert's family formed the Nkindongi sub-clan of the Iloitai Maasai—just one of numerous patriarchal sub-clans that make up the 17 tribes of the Maasai nation, which collectively extended through southern Kenya and northern Tanzania. Some customs, such as this stock-naming one, were shared by all Maasai, but others were peculiar to a tribal, as opposed to national, culture. Conversely, some practices—such as the removal of the two middle teeth in the lower jaw and the circumcision initiation rite—were respectively Nilotic and Hamitic in origin, thus representative of their broader ancestral mosaic.

All Maasai were bound by the fundamental belief that they were God's chosen people. They believed that all the cattle in the world belonged to them. In the beginning, Enkai, husband of the moon and Creator of all things, had sent cattle to the first Maasai from heaven, instructing them to love the livestock he provided as much as he himself loved them—and to this day, all Maasai continue to follow that teaching to the letter. Cattle are a central focus in their lives.

Catherine told us later that evening that the Maasai had 41 different words to describe the colour and markings of their dearly beloved livestock. The size of a herd was the measure of a man's wealth, as well as his family's traditional sole source of sustenance. In recent years the government had introduced *ugali*—a form of maize-meal—into their diet, but until then it had basically consisted of milk, meat and blood—the last being an emergency ration, drawn from a cow's jugular vein and consumed to provide a boost of protein and iron.

Although sheep and goats were usually slaughtered for food, cattle were reserved for rituals and ceremonial feasts. They were also used in the payment of fines. The clan system of the Maasai is believed to have its origin in the ownership of cattle, and the formal bride-price asked by the brothers and father of a bride invariably includes some cows. Robert had even given one to Catherine's brother, Mark, at the time of their wedding.

The task of milking cows fell to the women and every morning before the herd left the *enk'ang* to forage, and every afternoon when they came back to their thorny shrub-fenced enclosure, Catherine's mothers and sisters-in law collected enough for their families' needs in long, decorated calabashes. On our second afternoon at Narotian they teased me into giving it a go, but it was not as easy as it looked. Squeezing milk from a cow's udder was one thing—but actually getting it to go into the bottle-narrow neck of a hollowed-out gourd was damn-near impossible. It went everywhere but! Once everyone had had a good laugh, I was allowed to continue to spectate—with my camera—from the sidelines.

Memie, Narygunkishon and Meiyoki—the three 'sisters' sharing Catherine's *enk'ang*—were stunning, and photographing them, together with the 'mothers' (Kokoo and Mumai), was an absolute honour and a pleasure. Catherine had asked me to record portraits of all her family members for the book she was writing and the women could not have been more willing. It was a far cry from the usual response a tourist received from the Maasai, and they did not perceive my camera to be an intrusion. Moreover, it was a legitimate key into their world.

Wherever they moved, whatever they did, was a pure joy to behold. They were the most beautiful women—particularly Memie—and I was captivated by them completely. The graceful way in which they seemed to glide above the manure when they walked to and from the *enk'ang's* kraal; the way they carried themselves even when hauling jerry-cans of leaden water up from the stream really was poetry in motion. Their heads were perfectly shaved, their faces flawless, their ear lobes cut and stretched in keeping with tradition and decorated with magnificent beaded jewellery. So too their necks were encircled with banded discs of vivid colour. Their simple cotton togas were regal, their skin a luscious chocolate hue. They were exotic flowers, startling blooms on a veritable cactus of a landscape.

Photographing them inside their homes was a real challenge. Unlike Catherine's hut, a partition incorporated into the design stopped the cold wind and light from coming through the doorway. It was pitch dark inside and a single hole in the wall of the main chamber, barely the size of a dinner plate, was all I had to help me. Firelight was what the women generally worked by, but since the 'window' was shut to keep out flies, the smoke could not escape and thus the glowing hearth compounded rather than solved the problem.

Meiyoki's hut—the one she shared with her family and mother-in-law Mumai—was the most difficult to operate in. I felt like a great clumsy giant trying to move around in a shoe box. It was so cramped, just six-metres long, four wide, and only up to my shoulder in height. Its entrance was tunnel-shaped to keep out rain, and complemented the curve of the domed living area.

I think the seemingly impractical design of this style of hut was due to the fact that women were traditionally responsible for con-structing the family home. It was easier for them to pack leaves and mud around a frame they could reach across without too much trouble.

The origins of many Maasai customs or traditions were either lost or too complicated to explain, for when I questioned an action or practice, more often than not the response was just 'It is the Maasai way'. A lot of what I came to learn was therefore based on personal assumptions or interpretations by the individual I had quizzed.

Two days after we arrived, Robert, his brother James and nephew Loldudula returned to Narotian. It was definitely *not* the Maasai way to show through physical contact how pleased you were to see your wife after eight months' separation, so Robert just sort of nodded at Catherine, and she dutifully put a pot of water on the fire to boil for his tea. The only kisses you would ever see exchanged between men and women in public were those given and received by brothers and sisters.

James and Loldudula followed Robert into the hut and the six of us all sat around for a few hours talking. It was really great to see Bob again, and to finally meet the others, whom of course we'd heard so much about already from Catherine.

I felt very guilty, sitting there with 'the blokes', planning the adventure we had come this far to have. Poor Catherine, who was developing a strep-throat and head cold, would have just one night with her husband before they'd be apart for another week-long stint.

However she really felt about the situation in her heart, Catherine acknowledged that her husband, like all Maasai men, didn't like to spend a lot of time at home, and conceded he would be happier out there in the boonies with us, his brothers and fellow-members of his age-group, than stuck in the *enk'ang* with the women. The timing wasn't perfect, admittedly, but she could deal with that.

In Western terms, her generosity and understanding were over-whelming. In Maasai terms, it was, once again, just 'the Maasai way'.

Marriage and family were valued sanctions, but nothing would ever be as important as the age-set institution to a male Maasai. They even had an expression which, translated into English, placed the age-group equal to God.

In the course of his life, Robert would share every important initiation, ceremony, duty and privilege with the men of his generation or age-set. As pubescent boys, they had faced the rite of circumcision together. They had encouraged each other not to flinch, whimper or groan during the cutting, lest their reputation be ruined for ever. As initiates, they had roamed Maasailand side by side, hunting small birds to make their headdresses. As junior warriors, wearing their hair long and ochred, they had hunted a lion together and learned from their seniors what it was to be a man.

It was customary for members of the same age-set to graduate to manhood together, to forsake the itinerant lifestyle of the warrior and begin comparatively settled homelives. The sharing that had been so integral an element in their lives, now extended—in theory at least—to the sharing of wives.

An opportunity to relive the heady days of their junior warriorhood was one Maasai men would rarely pass on. Accompanying 'tourists' like Chris and me on an intimate trekking journey into Maasailand was the perfect sort of cash-paying occupation for guys like Robert and James, for it combined business and pleasure quite perfectly.

James lived with his wife and two children in another *enk'ang* at Imburapita, so we started our trek the next morning by walking over the hills and through the cool pockets of forest which lay between that region and Narotian. All other wildlife experiences we'd had to date paled, as we moved on foot past feeding zebra, impala and baboon. The little fear they exhibited was amazing, but indicative of the relationship Maasai had to their fauna. The lion—because of its role in determining a warrior's bravery and the threat it posed to domestic livestock—was the only animal these people traditionally hunted;[5] all other wildlife was protected, loved and respected.

I couldn't help but wonder how much that would change, if the government got its way and the Maasai of the Loita Hills were forced into an agricultural rather than pastoral lifestyle. They would surely have to kill, abhorrent as it seemed, in order to protect their fields and crops.

But for the time being, for however long that was, man and

---

[5] The government has outlawed the hunting of lions and continues to actively discourage the traditional period of warriorhood.

beast were allies and the Loitas was something of a sanctuary for both. Because of its relative isolation, the region had so far managed to avoid the Kenyan government's direct attention, so life—for the Maasai and the animal kingdom harboured there—remained largely unchanged.

When we reached Imburapita, we altered our plan for the first of many times. The donkeys we'd anticipated using to carry our camping kit and food through the Loita Hills were nowhere to be found. One of Robert's half-brothers—a lanky elder named Menya Le Kenya—occupied the only other hut in James' enk'ang, and he agreed to come with us and carry a load, as long as one of his age-set buddies could come along as well to keep him company. It was OK with Chris and me—especially me, given how much I despised burros. As long as we were able to keep the show on the road, we were happy.

So Robert, James, Loldudula, Menya Le Kenya, his friend Ole Kidinga (who also happened to be James' wife's brother) and Chris and I continued on our way to Tiamanagen. One big happy human family, sans jackass.

Our ultimate destination for the journey was, need I say—a mountain, but since it actually lay across the border in Tanzania, we were uncertain we would reach it. Apparently there had been a bit of elephant poaching and cattle rustling going on in the border area and there was a strong likelihood we'd be stopped from making the furtive border-crossing we hoped to effect by police. Or should I tell the truth and say their bullets? The way things were in East Africa, poachers—and possibly Maasai who looked ripe for a bit of a raid—were shot first, and asked questions later.

Since the collapse of the East African Community—the post-independence attempt to unify Kenya, Tanzania and Uganda—the Maasai's movements across the full extent of their realm had been restricted. The Kenyan-Tanzanian border ran straight through the middle of their traditional domain and governments on either side paid little heed to the fact that many family units had been cut off from one another since the common boundary's closure in 1977. It had been recently reopened of course, but only at two quite specific points, and everyone—even the Maasai—needed a passport to complete a legal crossing.

It was rarely possible for remote Maasai like the Nkindongi to ignore the artifical but strategically guarded boundary in order to cross where it was both expedient and convenient. Robert had agreed to give it a go, but if it looked at all dicey, we'd back off and return to Narotian. Chris and I could always climb Ol Doinyo Le Enkai when we went to Tanzania to have a go at Kilimanjaro.

Ol Doinyo Le Enkai—the Mountain of God—was sacred to all Maasai. It was not a peak they usually climbed, given that it was an active volcano, but it was one they regularly worshipped. It rose from the floor of the Great Rift Valley, a 'lone candle ... its constant rumbling thunder and lightning flames nothing less than the presence and power of God, Enkai, who is believed to live there and to whom the people bring sacrifices of lambs without spots'.[6]

Robert had checked with his local *laibon*—a prophet who lived near the Cathedral of the Seven Trees above Morijo—that we would not be breaking any tenant by climbing on the Mountain of God. It was the Maasai equivalent of the Buddhists' Mount Kailas in Tibet, and Chris and I were wary that it may have had the same 'off-limits' status. We knew other foreigners, including several vulcanologists, had climbed it before, but it was important to us to clear it with what amounted to an 'authority' or custodian of the Maasai culture first. The last thing we wanted was an untimely, wrathful eruption on our hands.

The last time it had actually 'gone off' was just six weeks previously, the same day we'd been climbing Thabana Nytlenyana

[6] From a book simply called *Maasai*, by Tepilit Ole Saitoti, a respected Maasai writer.

in Lesotho. According to the goss we'd heard at the weekly meeting of the Mountain Club of Kenya in Nairobi only the week before, it was still puffing and roaring like a steam train. Even if it proved impossible to climb, it would be an amazing thing to witness, regardless. We could stand—as the Maasai traditionally did—in its shadow, praying for cattle and children.

To avoid the 'meals-on-wheels syndrome', we hadn't brought the customary sacrificial lamb with us from Narotian, but intended buying one somewhere along the way to Ol Doinyo Le Enkai. Making a poor little defenceless critter walk all the way to its execution was awful; we'd been a part of that process before in Pakistan, *en route* to the Baltoro Glacier in the Karakorams. It was not something my fickle conscience could deal with. I could eat meat, but not if I regarded it as a friend beforehand.

Because of the border restrictions, Robert and his brothers had never physically undertaken a pilgrimage to their sacred mountain before, even though it was less than 100 kilometres as the crow flies from the Loitas. They had revered it in spirit, but not *in situ.* They were as excited by the prospect as we were—doubly so, because the route we would follow to reach the border would take in the villages of many friends and family members they had not seen in years. Robert had a sister in Tanzania as well, but they hadn't seen each other in an age and any chance of their paths crossing now was pretty slim.

Our guides and confidants looked resplendent in the afternoon light, their red togas flapping in the breeze, their aristocratic heads held high. Their spears glinted against the sun, their smooth legs glowed like polished ebony.

It took us about five hours to reach the village of Tiamanagen, slipping through the whisper of the long dry pasture grasses, passing beneath the murmur of the ancient, hallowed trees. Colobus monkeys rustled the forest canopies and startled plump turacos winged from bough to bough.

As the red sun sank low in the sky, children swished their family herds homeward. The sound of their dogs barking and cow bells tinkling quavered across the undulating lines of the landscape. The smell of smouldering dung tinged the air with all the richness of a melody. I could taste the notes of sweat streaming from my brow, feel the coda touch of fatigue in my limbs.

All these things, together, were the song of rural life. Through every sense I was filled with its symphony of joy. I had returned, once again, to the homeland in my heart.

As I watched the changing light, the children dancing through its beams, I realised just how much this instant meant to me. More important than any accolade I had ever received, more prized than any record, was this feeling—this knowing, deep within—that I had found the essence of my own existence.

It was scenes and moments such as these which had and would always define my life, remembered not in any logical order or chronological sequence, but drawn together like fragments in a kaleidoscope, forming patterns of great wonder and beauty.

I had not come to Africa to find another feather for my cap— I had come to see if I could find its soul. And here it was, ever so remarkably, right inside my own. We had become one, Africa and I, forever bound like lyrics to music, like photographs to memories.

A light rain began to fall shortly after we'd made camp for the night. The boys took refuge in an *enk'ang* just a short distance from our tent, vowing to return at seven the next morning. Chris and I cooked dinner, then settled down for a well-earned rest.

When I woke at daybreak, the hills were blanketed in mist. The smell of wet grass was almost too sweet to be true. I stood outside the tent for a while, listening to the stillness of the chilly winter dawn. It was amazing how much one sleep could change the way the world was. Yesterday had been unpleasantly warm; now my breath was visible on the coolness of the air.

Time was of little consequence to the Maasai, so 7am became 8 and 8 became 9. Each minute fed the fire of frustration smouldering inside my mind. I had never been able to shake my obsession with punctuality; it was the curse of the overdue child. Two weeks late at birth—and I'm still paying for it.

Patience was a concept I had spent my life trying to assimilate, but so far all attempts had been unsuccessful. Africa had too much of it, but none, it seemed, to give to me.

I was almost foaming at the mouth when the boys finally appeared. Apparently James had caused the hold-up through having decided one of the young girls in Tiamanangen would make a perfect second wife. With Menya le Kenya and Robert there for support, he had seized the moment to open a discussion on the issue with the father of his could-be bride. Negotiations would take some time, but that was OK, since the girl was only 11 years old, and not yet circumcised.

The day had already shed a number of its layers and was warming up to a sweat. There were many people on the trails we followed through the Loita Hills—women and young girls returning to their villages from a distant cousin's wedding celebration, junior warriors out on the prowl.

The virile *moran* were stunning in their youth—living works of art, all taut buttock and thigh. The way they wore their skimpy togas, the Rastafarian way they braided their shoulder-length hair with thin strips of leather and ochre, the way they stood on one leg, balanced and elegant like a siege of herons: I lost my heart to them a thousand times over.

James and Robert stopped to talk to everyone along the way—to ask them how things were in the forests at the end of the hills, where Kenya became Tanzania. By all accounts, it was a dangerous time to be thinking about crossing borders, and everyone advised against it.

By the time we reached the edge of the escarpment, we'd all agreed to forgo Ol Doinyo Le Enkai. Instead, we would trek off the highland and down to the Great Rift Valley floor, cross it, and climb up onto another massif called Champole to see if we couldn't at least get a better view of the Maasai's Mountain of God. So far, distance, heat and what we presumed to be a haze of dissipated smoke from the volcano had prevented us from seeing it.

Any disappointment we felt in falling short of our mark was quickly forgotten the following day. We broke camp early and trekked down the side of the Loita escarpment. Directly ahead of us, the perfect orb of a classic African sun was rising over distant plains. The twisted dance of the trees around me, their foliage spread to heaven like the open palms of a priest, were rendered static with the awe of dawn. There was not even a hint of a breeze and the temperature was rising with feverish speed.

The floor of the rift below us was breathtaking: so vast, so flat, so still. It was God's pallette, from whence all colour of the world had come, pure and bold and holy. Beneath the deepening blue of the sky we could see its yellow grasses flecked with gold, its pink-surfaced lakes lined with white soda, its vivid green swamps edged with solid black.

The air was alive over the land, shimmering hot, seething with the illusion of a giant mirage. It rose like the heat inside a sauna, stifling and lethargic.

Dust devils joined earth to sky, swirled by the random spirit of an impish air current. The columns vanished as quickly as they formed, then reappeared elsewhere on the great arid scape. When our paths crossed, we were drawn momentarily into the thrill of their vortex.

Thousands of zebras and wildebeest foraged in the brushstrokes of savanna which punctuated the barren plain. We walked between them, as if parting a sea teeming with minnows.

We marched for hours across the ever-changing hue of the Rift Valley floor, through dust so thick and dry it billowed like talcum underfoot. We marched for hours over drifts of blinding white soda, through acres of nothing but space. We marched for hours, but Champole never seemed to get any closer. The day grew hotter and longer, but there was nothing in this void to lend itself to a true sense of perspective or time. Even when it seemed as if we were directly beneath the mountain's great wrinkled brow, we were still several kilometres from its base.

We stopped to camp for the night when we hit the tail end of the Ewaso Ngiro River. If it weren't for the threat of hippos, we would have spent a few hours wallowing in its murky eddies, tepid as they were. Anything was better than the breathless, cease-less heat.

Loldudula, Robert and James went off to find the village of Champole. Menya Le Kenya and his mate wandered away to find firewood. Mountain or no Mountain of God, we would have our sacrificial lamb for tea.

Three teenage girls came down to our camp while the men were gone, wearing black robes and headbands fringed with chain. Their clothing marked them as women, very recently initiated by the rite of female circumcision.

Maasai clitoridectomies were not just a case of surgically excis-ing the clitoris; the labia minora and anterior two-thirds of the labia majora were removed as well. There was no such thing as anaesthetics in Maasailand and the operation, carried out in the far-from-sterile confines of a girl's mother's hut, was effected with a rusty old razor blade. Before they became available, a knife or sharpened stone had sufficed.

It made me sick to the stomach to think of it—not only the pain of such an operation, but the needlessness of it all. The Maasai didn't perform this rite for reasons of sexual fidelity; it was merely done to mark their passage to adulthood in a way that complemented the male initiation ceremony. There were surely better ways, but try telling that to a Maasai. The Kenyan government had outlawed the operation, but it was not something they were able to enforce.

The girls were charming, whispering and giggling to each other,

calling to Chris and flirting with their eyes. They were embold-
ened by the fact that he was a foreigner, but they sure made
themselves scarce when our Maasai crew returned!

It was well after 8pm when Loldudula made ready to kill the
kid he'd purchased from the village. There were no lambs in
Champole, but since it was really just a feed we were all after,
goat meat was deemed as good as any.

Robert called us from our tent to watch Loldudula suffocate
dinner. Using a firm hand, he grabbed the back and front legs of
the animal and forced it to gently lay on its side. He rested his
knee in the crook of its neck, and cupped his hand over its nostrils
and mouth. The kid barely struggled; it was more as if it were
being put to sleep, rather than killed, and I was surprised by how
humane the process seemed.

Three supposedly educated Maasai came down from the village
while the guys were cutting up the kid. They wore long pants and
shirts and the self-appointed spokesman of the 'committee' wore
thick-rimmed spectacles. His manner was officious, even if he
claimed no title. He demanded to know what we were doing in
'his' district and why we had set up camp on 'his' land. Where in
the name of Enkai had we come from, and where exactly did we
think we were going?

It took an hour, but the guys eventually convinced the pompous
interloper that we were not spies. When he demanded fees for
camping, they refused on our behalf, claiming that we were not
tourists either. We were Maasai just like them. One only had to
spend a day walking with us to prove that point. We were as
resilient and strong as they were, and Robert paid me the ultimate
compliment by nicknaming me *morani siangiki*, or 'warrior girl'.

We ate very late, then dozed for a few hours before getting up
at 3am for what we'd hoped would be a heat-beating early
morning start. In truth, the thermometer had barely budged since
the previous midday; in the lower altitude of the valley floor, the
change from day to night was a matter only of light and darkness,

not temperature. God knows what it must have been like down there in the summer months.

I woke Menya Le Kenya by pulling on his cut and stretched lobes. They felt gooey like the psychedelic 'Mister Twister' fishing lures Chris had in his tackle box at home. I had made a habit of teasing him by tugging on the wormlike lobes and looping them over the top of his ears, as was the Maasai fashion when one was caught without wooden stoppers or empty film canisters to plug up the slits.

Robert and James were already up and Ole Kidinga had 'won the straw' to stay behind and guard our camp. A *moran* from Champole village had agreed to lead us up the mountain to a suitable vantage point, and when he appeared just after four o'clock, we set off beneath the sallow light of the setting moon.

We moved in silence, skirting the great base of the mountain all the way around to its southern end. It was just starting to get light when we reached the point from which we would climb. There was no trail, and I doubted anyone had scaled the mountain to its summit from where our 'guide' had chosen to ascend; it looked impossible. Still, we tried.

Menya Le Kenya was constantly tripping as he caught the wide toe of his 'thousand-milers'[7] on exposed thornbush roots. The volcanic scree was loose and rough and difficult to climb on, but the way of the scrub was even nastier. It tore at our clothes and flesh. The guys had insisted on bringing their spears with them, but in this terrain they were proving quite a hindrance. I had visions of them all, impaled like exotic shish-kebabs, lying in a pile at the bottom of a hidden gully.

After an hour we reached a narrow but prominent knoll and called it quits. It was as good a vantage point as any. I pulled out the binoculars and looked south. I could not see the Mountain of God. The eastern sky was overcast and the light still a little dim,

---

[7] Sandals made from the recycled tread of a tyre.

but there was nothing even vaguely suggestive of a volcano in sight. The boys joked that it must have blown itself up completely. They were at a loss to explain its absence from the horizon otherwise. I guessed the smoke from Ol Doinyo Le Enkai was keeping it screened; it was still too far away to see through such a haze.

Directly below where we were sitting, and wholly within Tanzania, was Lake Natron, one of the many famous soda lakes of the Great Rift Valley system. I scanned its nearest shallow waters through the binoculars, hoping to see some of the flamingoes which were said to feed on the algae and insect lava in such lakes. We were still a good kilometre above and away from the northern extent of the lake, and all the binocular's magnification revealed was a vast patch of boring-looking reeds bristling the still shadowed surface.

As I was staring, disappointed, over the dull waterbody, the sun rose above the shoulder of Champole behind me, and diffused light spread like honey over the floor of the valley below. A single beam shot out from a bow in the mountain's profile like a flaming arrow and sped along the gunpowder edge of the lake. The surface exploded with a wild red flash of fire. Every stiff reed was ignited like a match.

I sharpened the focus on the binoculars. My heart leapt into my mouth. They were not reeds, but flamingoes! Thousands of them! Tens of thousands of them! I couldn't stop myself from screaming.

Tears were rolling down my cheeks; it was so sudden, so glorious a moment. It was as if a curtain had opened, revealing an enormous stage awash with prima ballerinas. They rose and fell, like a wave of fans in a stadium; they danced like a flurry of confetti at a wedding. They swirled and twirled before my eyes, all giddy grace and beauty.

The light reached right across the valley and seeped like a liquid dye up through the base of the distant Loita escarpment. I passed the binoculars to Chris, so he too could see what I was seeing.

The guys were in hysterics over my reaction to the scene, but could barely contain themselves once they had had their turn to witness its magnified magnificence. We couldn't get off the mountain and down to the water's edge fast enough!

We slid and slopped our way out across the exposed mudflats of northern Lake Natron. There was nothing to hide behind, so we just moved as slowly and quietly as we could towards the feeding birds. They soon accepted our presence and stopped shying from it. I hunkered down with the boys and the binoculars a good fifty metres from the shore, but Chris moved even closer to film the grand performance.

The pale pink flamingoes stalked along with their heads bowed low, as if battling a strong wind. They did not stop still to feed, but ate on the run, sucking up molluscs, crustaceans and other organic particles hidden in the mud. There were so many of them nesting on the briny lake that when you looked beyond its edge, foreshortening caused them to appear as a solid wall of coral pink.

An island of cormorants held court in the centre of the grouping nearest us. They seemed to be transfixed, as we were, by the splendour of the ballet. Overhead, two clouds of pelicans circled, soaring on the belly of a thermal. They kept their wings stationary and spiralled higher and higher until they were just as tiny as snowflakes in the sky. Thirty pure white swans, like a line of bows on the tail of an invisible kite, moved in slow motion through the crystal air.

At around 10.30am we reluctantly started back to our camp by the river on the far side of Champole. We were desperate for shade and water, having run out of both the hour before. It was a long, hot hike, but Chris and I were so full of the moment we walked with a spring in our step.

Back on the banks of the Ewaso Ngiro, wolfing down big mugs of leftover goat-fat broth, Robert and James suggested we were ready for the ultimate Maasai walking experience. Over the past

One of the vents inside the crater of Ol Doinyo Le Enkai.

Left to Right, Robert, me, James and Loldudula on the edge of the Loita escarpment overlooking the Great Rift Valley.

Chris and a Dust Devil about to collide on the Rift Valley floor.

The Furtwangler Glacier inside the crater of Kilimanjaro, glistens in the late afternoon sunlight.

Ice formations on the summit ridge of Kilimanjaro with Mawenzi in the background.

Chris and James in the Rift Valley, en route to Champole Mountain.

Inside the crater of
Kilimanjaro.

Zemnesh, Asbrber,
Yeashreg and Mukatier
inside their family
hut in Arkwasiye
village, Ethiopia.

Getenet Akalu (centre) and our two scouts, Belai Gadaum and Yeshue Tenew on top of Ras Dejen, Ethiopia.

Sorrel with a group of friends in Arkwasiye village, Ethiopia. (The hat is a chel'ada Baboon hat.)

Dihwara village en route to Dirni in the Simien Mountains, Ethiopia.

Sunset over the low-
lands below the Simien
escarpment, Ethiopia.

Saha, the Simien
Mountains, Ethiopia.

Getenet Akalu at the
Chennek camp, Simien
Mountains, Ethiopia.

Village girl herding
cows in Nariya Mikael
village, Ethiopia.

Textures of Africa.

eleven years they had spent many days trekking with foreigners, but never had any agreed to move through their country at night. Would we dare to be the first?

We had already trekked some 30 kilometres that day, but Chris and I could not resist the challenge. We rested for a few hours, then at 4.30pm set out to retrace our steps across the Great Rift Valley floor.

We walked straight into the sun for the first two hours and reached the foot of the Loita escarpment just on nightfall. James pointed out a set of lion prints, as big and deep as cake tins in the talcy dust, but reassured me we had nothing to fear, so long as we stayed close together. Robert thought it was very funny that I was afraid, especially in the august company of so many proven warriors.

The Maasai only resorted to using torches on rough terrain, so when we moved through the desert of low thorn and dwarf boab skirting the base of the escarpment, we did so in complete inky darkness. There was no moon to guide us and what little light the stars afforded was quickly extinguished by a bank of cloud rolling in from the west.

At first, the experience was terrifying. Chris and I floundered and stumbled over every little ripple, root and rock in the landscape. There was no path to follow—Robert was letting some secret sixth sense take the lead.

We soon got the hang of it—it was all just a matter of self-trust, of mind over matter. We had to feel the terrain, become one with the earth and move with it, not through it, like fallen leaves in a stream. It was an extraordinary sensation: an art which I will always be grateful to the Maasai for sharing with me, even if I never undertake such a journey again.

By ten-thirty, we were all in a trance. There was still no wind or respite from the heat, still no moon lightening the sky. Fatigue gave way to exhaustion, but there was no stopping what we had begun.

At midnight we began ascending the escarpment. A brush fire, lit to encourage new growth, filled the air with the rank odour of charred grass. The flames formed a huge ring on the mountainside, a burning brand on the flank of Maasailand. The seared ground lay black and smouldering.

A solid bronze wedge of a moon appeared on the opposite horizon, surrounded by a perfect circle of stars. We rose with it, surely, steadily upward. The fickle clouds were clearing, but we could feel nothing of the breeze that moved them.

It was 3am by the time we reached the top of the Loita escarpment. A thousand metres of altitude made a big difference to the temperature, and goosebumps formed beneath my sweat. We were utterly spent. It was difficult to tell exactly how far we'd walked in the last 24 hours, but it was well over 60 kilometres for sure. Every fibre of every muscle ached and throbbed.

It was an initiation, our own rite of passage into the Maasai world, one which would bind us to the men we'd shared the journey with forever. They could speak of little else during the long two-day trek back to Narotian, and it was a hell of an honour to hear them talk of our fortitude to others, as if it were equal to their own.

We hadn't reached the holy Mountain of God, but there would be opportunities for all of us to do so, sooner or later. For the time being there was more than enough to celebrate without the glory of a summit. No mountain, no matter how sacred, would ever be as prized as friendships, and those we'd formed with Robert and his brothers were golden ones indeed.

MOUNT KENYA AND THE
AVENUE OF VOLCANOES

MORE THAN A MONTH would pass before Chris and I
were able to make a second attempt on Ol Doinyo
Le Enkai. We stayed on at Catherine and Robert's
enk'ang for a while, making day treks a little closer to home.
We lobbed down to Morijo and met Robert's mother, his other
wife, adopted brother and numerous other members of the
extended Rerente family. I couldn't get over the striking resem-
blance many of them bore to each other; they either had pre-
potent genes, these Nkindongi Iloitai Maasai, or they'd cottoned
on to the cloning thing a few generations before us. Menya Le
Kenya was a dead ringer for his own birth mother and I was
agape at the similarity between one of Robert's brothers and a
particularly handsome, apparently unrelated child in residence
at Morijo. The father-son bloodline *was* there of course, but

illicitly so, and to suggest as much—even unwittingly—was something of a *faux pas* on my part. The fireside subject was very quickly changed indeed.

We roamed the forests and scoured the plains, followed honey guide birds in search of hives, learned how to throw a Maasai spear and picked up on a few local bush remedies. Every tree and plant in Maasailand was good for something; in fact the words for tree and medicine were one and the same. They even had a toothbrush tree, which was so effective it rivalled any Western brand I'd ever used. The slightly acidic sap emitted from a cut twig and rubbed directly on the teeth was better than your average fluoride treatment at the dentist.

We met up with some clients from a friend's safari company and hitched a ride back into Nairobi on their re-supply vehicle. Steve Amezdroz—the executive producer from Beyond assigned to our proposed television documentary series—flew into town with the news that Channel Nine had signed a presale agreement. He was on his way to the UK and the USA to try and get similar interests vested there, but needed more information and some sort of documentation from us before he could make a viable presentation. He had sold the series concept to Channel Nine on the basis of our reputation and the network's reaction to our *60 Minutes* profile story, but he needed more than that to win the big boys overseas.

We spent the next three days in Steve's hotel room, trying to put our ideas and vision into words. When all that was over, we ventured out to climb Logonot in the Rift Valley, then headed off to Mount Kenya—the second-highest peak on the continent. Iian Allan, the director of Tropical Ice, a safari company which specialised in organising mountain-based adventures, had invited us to join one of his scheduled trips up Point Lenana,[1] so despite our

---

[1] The most accessible of Mount Kenya's three summits and the one most people climb as it requires little or no experience. The other two are slightly higher, but every route demands a certain level of technical rock-climbing expertise.

anxiousness to get to Tanzania to climb Ol Doinyo Le Enkai, we signed on.

Clive Ward, a pipe-smoking, wiry middle-aged safari guide from the 'old school', led the expedition, assisted by a young woman from California named Tina. She was a living Barbie Doll, tall and blonde and totally lacking animation. She was working a season for Tropical Ice—not for wages, just for the chance to see some of the country—but she didn't seem to be making much of the opportunity at all. In fact, she appeared to be totally bored by the whole East African experience.

Together with the two clients—a retired couple from Washington named Herman and Jean—we drove out to the village of Chogoria, intent on climbing Lenana via the glaciated Gorges Valley route. It was a no-expense-spared sort of journey: gourmet meals, lavish picnics, an army of porters to carry everything, hot water and tea brought to your tent first thing in the morning—the works. After ascribing to the do-it-yourself and spend-as-little-as-you-possibly-can ethic all my life, I thought I'd died and gone to heaven.

Mount Kenya was a monumental peak, the true monarch of East Africa's mountains. It was a singular entity 5199 metres high and 100 kilometres in diameter, an extinct volcano with lush camphor and cedar forests enveloping its base. Impenetrable jungles of bamboo crept up the sides of its great hulking form, and moorlands of tussock grass dotted with giant heather and groundsel draped its solid shoulders like an imperial stole. A necklace of sparkling topaz lakes circled the nape of the massif, which was further crowned by a formidable realm of rock spires, towers and turrets, giant boulders, glaciers and scree. It was worshipped by the local Kikuyu people, who believed that their God dwelt amid the summit peaks, and revered by climbers the world over.

Chris came down with some mystery virus on the second evening of our trek up the eastern side of the great mountain. It

was the first time either of us had suffered any sickness whatsoever on the expedition, and in spite of all our first-aid training, we couldn't work out what was wrong with him. Assuming
it was just some 24-hour bug, he persevered, and pushed on
up to Lake Ellis—a remote site hidden in the lower heath-
choked folds of Mount Kenya. Even a spot of fishing, yielding
two record-breaking trout, failed to lift his flagging spirits. By
nightfall, he felt too ill even to taste the spoils of his favourite
sport.

Assuming he'd contracted some peculiar 48-hour lurgy, he continued with us up to Hall Tarns camp. It was the most magnificent place on the entire mountain, with spectacular views in every
direction, but even they failed to raise his temperament or lower
his temperature.

The antibiotics and Panadine weren't working; the codeine in
the latter was only adding to his woes. The 48 hours became 72.

Chris thought another day would do it and then he'd be fine,
but in choosing to take it, it meant we'd have to split from the
Tropical Ice crew. They were sticking to an itinerary which lacked
the flexibility of our own, and delaying their ascent and subsequent traverse of the mountain would throw their whole scheduled program out of whack.

Just in case Chris did not improve, I decided to climb Lenana
with the rest of the group, and return to the Hall Tarns camp
alone. If Chris was better the next day, I would climb the summit
peak again with him; if not, we'd simply back-track to Chogoria
and get to Nairobi as quickly as possible.

It was bitterly cold on the morning of the group ascent. We
were woken at 2am, but no amount of clothing or hot cups of
tea seemed to warm me. When we finally got moving on the
sliding scree trail, the pace was so slow I still couldn't raise my
core temperature, and before long I was feeling really bad. I came
so close to passing out, I had to sit down on a rock for a while.
When I called out to alert Clive, my voice was not my own. It

was so distant; so strange. It took every mental resource I owned to stop myself from fainting.

Nothing like that had ever happened to me on a mountain before, and I couldn't understand why it was occurring now. It was definitely not an altitude-related symptom; I had no headache, no nausea, no nothing, so I figured I would be OK if I could only warm myself up. It didn't even cross my mind that I may have been coming down with the same virus Chris was enduring—I just tried to ignore it, and pressed on. I was just incredibly cold, that was all, cold to the bone.

Gradually the sky changed from black to violet to blue. We watched the sunrise from a ridge some 300 metres below, and several kilometres away from Point Lenana. Just seeing it was enough to take my temperature up a notch or two, and the rest of the climb was much more enjoyable. By the time I reached the top, I was feeling 100 per cent.

I wish I could have said the same for Chris, but down below at Hall Tarns, a mere speck on the landscape from the high aerie of Lenana, he was utterly miserable. When I got back down at 11am, he was still wrapped up in his sleeping cocoon shivering.

Later that afternoon, two other Australian trekkers rocked into the camp site. I went over to say G'day and realised Chris and I had met the couple before—in Nepal, right in the heart of Yeti and Everest country, in a little mountain chalet in the village of Dole. It was too incredible for words, and Patricia—who just so happened to be a doctor—remembered that Chris had been in a pretty sorry state then, as well.

Trish was not too sure what was ailing the poor boy because he'd complicated his symptoms by taking too much codeine. Since whatever it was had stopped him from smoking, we joked that it was obviously something life-saving and not, as I had secretly feared, a life-threatening disease. The good doctor's husband, Laurie—a comic by nature and an elephant trainer by trade—wandered over to console Chris, leaving Trish and me free to talk at length about the wimp nature of men. Us girls were made of much sterner stuff by far; you wouldn't catch us playing the woose when there were mountains to climb! No way! We'd be up there giving them a go, no matter how pathetically sick we were. Us girls—we had muscles on our shit, we did!

Pride always comes before a fall. A week later, I was laid up in bed with a Mac truck parked on my chest. I had pneumonia.

Confinement bothered the hell out of me, and everyone else besides. In the absence of mountains, I started climbing the frigging walls. Paul and Susan's home was an absolute paradise, but after five days it really started closing in around me. The security bars on all the windows only contributed to my feelings of entrapment.

When the condition of my lungs improved, I escaped to the city for an afternoon with Chris and Glen—a dear friend of ours, who supplied the necessary get-away car. I lasted about ten minutes on the streets and needed another two days in bed to recover.

I just didn't have any strength at all, and the smallest exertion completely wiped me out. The doctor treating me made me promise I wouldn't go near a mountain for a month, but two weeks away from my beloved peaks was more than I could bear. I lied to Chris that I'd been given the all-clear, and we made ready for the Tanzanian leg of our Summit Safari.

Because of the delay in our master plan, Paul was able to clear his slate at the High Commission, take a week and a half off and join us on our trip to Ol Doinyo Le Enkai. On Saturday 11 September, we loaded up his tiny short-wheel-base Suzuki 4WD with everything we could possibly need, filled the tank with petrol, and trundled off to the Kenyan border together.

Paul drove like a maniac down the 104, and we reached Namanga in a little over two hours. Hordes of people roamed the no-man's-land between Kenya and Tanzania: truck drivers, tourists, sharp dudes wearing flairs and fake name-brand shades (the ubiquitous money changers) and easily a hundred Maasai women selling badly made jewellery and used beaded calabashes. Several persistent pedlars were blown away when I greeted them in Maa, their language, and introduced them to *'morani sapuk'*— my 'big warrior' husband. As a result, I was offered very special rates on their wares. One woman even approached me with an opportunity to short-cut adoption procedures: if I could cough up the necessary barter—my underpants—she would give me her beautiful 10-month-old baby. I guess it was a fashion thing—after all, I *was* wearing Bendons. I wondered how supermodel Elle 'I don't think you should read anything you haven't written your-self' Macpherson would construe the deal?

All was clearly not well in the Nation of Nyerere[2]. If this bizarre barter was an indication of hard times, then Tanzania had been bought to its knees. When a woman is prepared to give up her baby for a pair of undies she thinks she could possibly sell, it makes you wonder where the aid dollars have been going all these years. Tanzania received more of them than any other nation on the continent, and yet its people continued to suffer more than most.

In spite of all the foreign dollars it earned through tourism or procured through aid, Tanzania was a total economic mess. According to the annual World Development Report, it was the second-poorest country in the world. Only Mozambique had a lower GNP.

Very few of the donated dollars actually made it into the pockets of Joe-average. Money earned through tourism was rarely ploughed back into the potentially viable industry. Most of it (if you could believe all current speculation) was ferreted away into individual Swiss bank accounts.

The well-intentioned policies of Nyerere's radical socialism—

[2] Julius Nyerere was Tanzania's first president, from 1961 to 1985. In foreign capitals they called him 'the conscience of black Africa'.

which banned government ministers and party officials from receiving more than one salary, or holding shares or directorships in companies, lest they develop into an exploitative class—had gone out the window. For all the years he led by example, drawing a presidential salary of just US$6000 and travelling economy class on state visits, his peers and successors had succumbed to greed.

Three decades of dogmatic socialist rule had failed to improve the lot of those who'd endured it. Their agricultural production was stagnant, their transport systems dysfunctional and their industries were limping along at well under 50 per cent capacity. With no economic incentives in the system, socialism had turned good old African stoicism into apathy.

The situation was visibly bleak; to add insult to injury, the nation was currently blighted by drought. We couldn't believe how dry and barren the land was between the border and Arusha—the former headquarters of the East African Community and present-day 'safari capital' of Tanzania. There was nothing holding the topsoil in place; it had turned to dust long ago, and now it billowed in great clouds, swirled by a hot, relentless wind. There were people in that godforsaken landscape, people and goats, both wandering in search of food and water. It was a vision I'd seen countless times before—on news bulletins and Freedom from Hunger campaigns.

The land immediately near Arusha was unbelievably lush by comparison, even if the town itself was largely down at heel. The time it took for the scenery to change from insidious to magnificent was no longer than your average television commercial break.

All around the base of imposing Mount Meru, which cast its great shadow over Arusha, volcanic soils and an equatorial microclimate ensured fertility, as did the absence of livestock. The mountain and its surrounds formed a small national park, so very little of the land within it had been cleared. We detoured up to the entrance gate, driving through the best forest I'd yet seen in Africa.

Mount Meru was awesome to behold; a quarter of a million years ago an eruption had completely blown away its entire eastern flank. What remained of the volcano's rim enclosed the forest growing in the floor of the ancient crater like an amphitheatre. The park gate was situated on the eastern, open side, so as we approached it we looked directly onto the daunting arc of an unbroken, 2000-metre-high scree wall.

On route to Arusha, we'd decided not to head directly to Ol Doinyo Le Enkai. Paul had offered to make an overnight stop at the base of Kilimanjaro, so we could stash the gear and supplies Chris and I would need for that climb at a fellow Mountain Club of Kenya member's home in Moshi. We'd sleep the night there, then in the morning drive west, picking up specific directions for Ol Doinyo Le Enkai on our way back through Arusha. It was only a few hundred kilometres out of the way.

I was starting to think the guy was a saint; his goodness knew no bounds. It was wholly appropriate, given that we'd missed our chance with the Maasai, that we were destined to climb the Mountain of God with him.

Finding someone in Arusha who could accurately describe the way to Ol Doinyo Le Enkai was a challenge in itself. It was not a place many people went to—and then, it seemed, they only ever did with a peer or guide who was intimately familiar with the surrounding terrain. The route was notoriously vague beyond its unsignposted turn-off from the trans-Tanzanian section of the 104 Highway, and the best instructions we could muster, devoid of even relative distances, were 'cross the river, but whatever you do don't turn left' followed by 'cross the river, turn left'.

But we were in trouble well before the appearance of any damn river in the landscape: we missed the initial turn-off completely. We flew through the village of Mto Wa Mbu, climbed the Rift Valley escarpment and motored halfway to Ngorongoro Crater before realising we'd gone too far. We wasted half an hour back-tracking to Mto Wa Mbu, and another full one quizzing the locals for directions.

Africans never wanted to disappoint you by saying they didn't know the way to a particular destination, so more often than not they sent you off on an admittedly well-intentioned wild-goose chase. Eventually, after asking three dozen people and getting three dozen different sets of instructions, we headed out of town and chanced finding the route ourselves.

There was actually an array of optional tracks, but we soon figured they all followed the same course, roughly, coming together like the fraying strands of a rope. Paul swapped from one set of wheel ruts to another, but never once changed speed.

We bolted due north, straight down the barrel of the Great Rift Valley. The bulldust was like nothing I'd ever seen before—when we slowed down even slightly, it caught up with us, completely swallowing the car and forcing it to a standstill. Visibility was reduced to zero until the talcy dust settled. It was stinking hot, but the air-conditioner was really eating up the juice, so we turned it off for as long as we could bear it, playing a game of 'chicken' with the windows for ventilation. That soon stuffed their automatic winder function—like every other moving part and orifice in the vehicle, it became clogged with dust.

It was so barren out there we could scarcely believe the region was inhabited, not only by wildlife, but by people. We passed a few isolated and totally depressing settlements and several herd boys out in the middle of nowhere with their goats. River beds were drier than a dingo's armpit, so god knows where they were heading in search of water. Their only hope lay underground.

Vegetation was minimal, but great gaggles of Thomson's gazelle and zebra took flight as we bounded past their hides of withered thornbush. There were giraffe as well, hanging out in groups of three, tearing leaves from the faded acacias with their Mick Jagger lips and foot-long tongues. They were so tall, so fantastic, like hybrid sea-grass swaying on a current or coral polyps craning for the sun.

Because of their size and stride the speed of their gait was deceptive. They were capable of moving at almost 50 kilometres an hour, but watching them gallop was like seeing a film sequence played in slow motion.

Further along, as we neared the 'Avenue of Volcanoes', we spotted a great herd of wildebeest. It was difficult to look at this particular species and not feel a certain sense of divine humour. As if constructed from a bunch of leftover parts, the poor beast was even more comical and bizarre than Picasso's imaginary bull in *Guernica*.

Ol Doinyo Le Enkai finally came into view at around two in the afternoon. Its shape was perfect, rising abruptly from the dead-flat landscape, compelling our every attention. There was no actual smoke plume rising from it, but its very dramatic, powerful form engendered excitement in all of us.

Even from relatively close quarters it looked impossibly steep; over 2000 vertical metres of hideous bare scree and grey ash. There appeared to be nothing in the way of vegetation on its sides and sodium carbonate, emitted at every eruption, streaked the summit area with white. It was utterly daunting, and in its shadow I felt not only insignificant, but completely incompetent as well. I felt defeated by it, long before we even reached its base.

The road skirted the Mountain of God at a respectful distance, then suddenly shot off away from it. We kept going, expecting to find a left-hand turn somewhere, but when none appeared we started to panic. We must have gone too far ...

We backtracked a good 20 kilometres, but there were no other distinct roads—and certainly none sign-posted in the anticipated manner. There was supposed to be a small settlement at the foot of the mountain and a couple of commercial campsites thereabouts, but we couldn't work out where, and feared we'd end up back in Kenya if we kept following the main drag. Paul scooped the dust away from the dash and announced we had just half a tank of petrol left—enough to get back out to Mto Wa Mbu, but nary a drop to waste going back and forth across the rift looking for the access road to Le Enkai. We were getting low on drinking water as well. Reluctantly, we retracked our tyre tread all the way back to the 104.

We reached Mto Wa Mbu for the third time that day just on sunset. We were covered in dust from head to toe and the car looked as if had been to hell and back. We were totally deflated, but determined to have one last crack at locating the right access route.

In the morning we fuelled up the meagre 40-litre tank and bought an extra 20-litre jerry can of petrol to cover every eventuality. By chance, we met a bloke at the service station who knew the route well. Apparently you *did* reach the base of Le Enkai by driving away from it! If we had continued just five or ten kilometres further from the point where we'd opted to backtrack, we would have 'crossed the river and turned left' and found our signpost leading the way to the elusive Maasai settlement beneath the Rift Valley escarpment directly below the Serengeti Plain.

It took the better part of a day to get there, nonetheless. We bogged twice, hanging the diff on a compacted island of fine powdery silt, the four wheels spinning free. On the first occasion I procured a spear from a passing warrior to dig the vehicle off its pedestal while the boys hauled rocks up from a nearby river bed to lay beneath the wheels. It was hard work in the heat of the day and we'd no sooner gained mobility before the same thing happened again. Fortunately this time, though, a white saviour in a Land Rover appeared from nowhere and dragged us out of trouble with a winch.

We were all exhausted by the time we limped into the campsite, but before collapsing made arrangements with the camp manager to hire a guide for our proposed climb up Ol Doinyo Le Enkai. We agreed to make an early start of it to beat the brunt of the daily heat, and set Paul's watch alarm for 2.30am.

After what felt like a total of ten minutes' sleep, the three of us were up and at it again, getting ready for the day's action. A young *moran* came down with Phillip, the camp manager, and in the sallow glow of his torch we were introduced to our guide. Phillip decided we needed security—someone to mind the car while we climbed the mountain—and volunteered his own services ... for a price, of course.

We left the campsite at 3am and drove along an obscure track to the western side of the mountain. It was an abysmal piece of road, worse for the fact that Paul's shock absorbers had died the previous day. There was not a great deal of clearance between the chassis of the car and *terra firma*, and every rock, bump, hole and ditch jarred and jolted every bone, nerve and fibre of our beings.

It was still pitch dark at 4am when we started climbing. We moved on a trail lined with thick tussock grass, along a sort of raised ridge. We were, at first, oblivious to the great drop-off on either side of the little-used route, but when light slowly crept into the sky we realised just how exposed the track was. Looking ahead was even more discouraging; it seemed as if we'd barely covered a quarter of the distance, and the route up was far steeper than the territory already covered.

At six we stopped for a breather and watched the sun rise over the vast Serengeti. The endless plain was completely devoid of trees, its hardpan layers of volcanic carbonatite ash impenetrable to all but the most shallow-rooted grasses. The only movement across it came in the form of Ol Doinyo Le Enkai's shadow, spreading like a stain across the valley floor, up the escarpment and far out into the middle of the awesome, silent scape. I tried to imagine I was watching the annual migration of wildlife for which the park was famous. In my mind's eye I pictured the greatest concentration of large mammals on earth. I saw the dust, swirled by the hooves of one and a half million wildebeest, I was dizzied by the stripes of 200 000 zebras, spellbound by the beauty of wave upon wave of leaping gazelle, chilled by the pride of 3000 lions that followed in the wake of the exodus.

Back in the real world Chris was tugging on my T-shirt, anxious to be on the move himself. It was stinking hot already, even in the shade; the more climbing we could complete before the sun came over the shoulder of the mountain, the better off we'd be.

The June eruption had severely damaged the established route up to the summit and we were very glad to have brought our climbing rope with us. We were going to make good use of it on the way down! The slope was growing steeper by the minute— the scree finer, deeper and more demanding. Before long we were clambering on all fours, sliding two steps backwards for every clawing move forward. It was like trying to climb an endless sand dune.

The vile, poisonous smell of rotten egg gas grew more and more pungent as we neared the crater. It was escaping from small vents and fissures everywhere. The heat was not just coming from the atmosphere now; it was radiating from the very bowels of the earth, bubbling in the form of lava less than a hair's-breadth beneath our feet.

Enkai's first deep rumble scared the hell out of me. For all the world, I thought the volcano was going to blow. I grew accustomed to the sound, eventually, but it was never anything less than disconcerting—a constant reminder of not only the presence of God, but the devil himself as well.

Right on 9am we scrambled over the last baked rib of the western flank of the mountain, dragged ourselves up onto the rim and stared down into the crater bowl. It was incredible; not the bubbling fiery mass I had anticipated, but a wholly alien environment straight from the realm of a celluloid sci-fi.

The floor of the crater was little more than 20 metres below the lip of its encircling wall. It was dead flat and stark white from

all the sodium carbonate emitted and deposited during past erup-
tions. Three sweeping cone 'chimneys' rose from the basin, each
encrusted with vivid yellow- and rust-hued sulphur crystals. Wisps
of steam curled from cracks within the ash and a large vent in
the middle of the crater alternately belched and roared. The
intense heat escaping from it was visible, shimmering the air
above.

Chris filmed from the rim, then followed Paul, the *moran* and
me down onto the crater floor. Our first few steps were tentative
indeed; the surface was patchy with exotic flowers of lava little
more than a day or two young, and much older welts of dry
flaking skin just barely concealing the hot thick 'mud' layered
beneath. The first time my foot-fall collapsed a thinner section of
this crust, I screamed at the top of my lungs. I was sure I was
going to extract a charred stump from the ooze. Fortunately the
lava was cooler than I imagined and my reflexes sharp as a tack:
I only melted the edge off the sole of one shoe!

I could not resist the magnetic pull of the main vent; I had to
get near it for a closer look. Paul and I moved slowly towards the
great gaping hole, while Chris kept the video camera rolling.

The heat was incredible, moist and strong and tangible. Our
guide joined us on the lip of the cavernous stairwell to hell and
the three of us tiptoed around its opening.

Suddenly the wind changed direction. The great wall of heat
swung around and slapped straight into us. We dropped like nine-
pins down the raised embankment of the vent. The sheer force,
to say nothing of the temperature, was absolutely terrifying. If
you had a heat-resistant suit and a tad more derring-do, you could
have thrown yourself at the hole and floated above it forever,
buoyed by the strength of the up-draft. Dressed as we were—Paul
in shorts, me in thin pants and the *moran* bare-bottomed beneath
his token red toga—we couldn't get within cooee of the furnace
opening for more than a second or two at a time.

From where Chris was watching and filming us, it must have

looked outrageous. Each time we crawled up the shielding side of the vent he said we liquefied in the vapour; our bodies appeared to melt and drip as if they were effigies fashioned from candle wax. Our heads were detached from our torsos and our limbs ran like oil over water.

Eventually we wandered away from the main vent to explore a few of the lesser volcanic flues rising from the crater floor. Each niche was encrusted with sulphur, turned into an exotic little shrine of orange and yellow stalactites and stalagmites. Even though the openings were much smaller they were just as blistering and pungent, and the hanging calcified formations were way too hot to touch.

By eleven o'clock we were all starting to feel a little queasy from the fumes. It was time to return to planet earth. We climbed out of the crater and stood on its rim for a few final moments and one last long look.

Way in the distance, hundreds of kilometres away, I could see another volcano. Its glistening snow-capped summit was hovering above the horizon like a spaceship, separated from its own earthly moorings by an illusion of haze lying over the plains. It was Kilimanjaro, the beacon of Africa, the highest peak on the entire continent. It was dormant, yet wholly sublime, a fitting mate for this other-worldly Mountain of God. They faced each other, like opposing kings on a chess board, incorporeal and sacred. We were but pawns in their presence: inconsequential, expendable, profane.

Never had I felt so humbled by a view.

KILIMANJARO

FINALLY STANDING ON the summit of Ol Doinyo Le Engai was really something, but the challenges surmounted to reach the lofty hot-spot really paled once we began descending it. With the full heat of the day only marginally lower in ferocity and temperature than that emanating from the crater vents, we set off from the rim in a sweat. The loose scree, stirred as we plunged downhill, sent up choking smoke-signals of soda, the wind blowing the fine particles into our eyes, noses, ears and mouths. Our throats were quickly parched, and we soon ran out of drinking water.

The technique we'd employed to climb the Mountain of God was difficult in reverse and we were glad to have a well-anchored rope to hang onto on several of the steeper, more exposed pitches. Where the gradient eased off slightly, we were able to glissade on our butts. I was pleased I hadn't traded off my undies, and felt sorry for our bare-bummed *morani*; the talus was sharp and since my own trousers were shredded just half an hour into

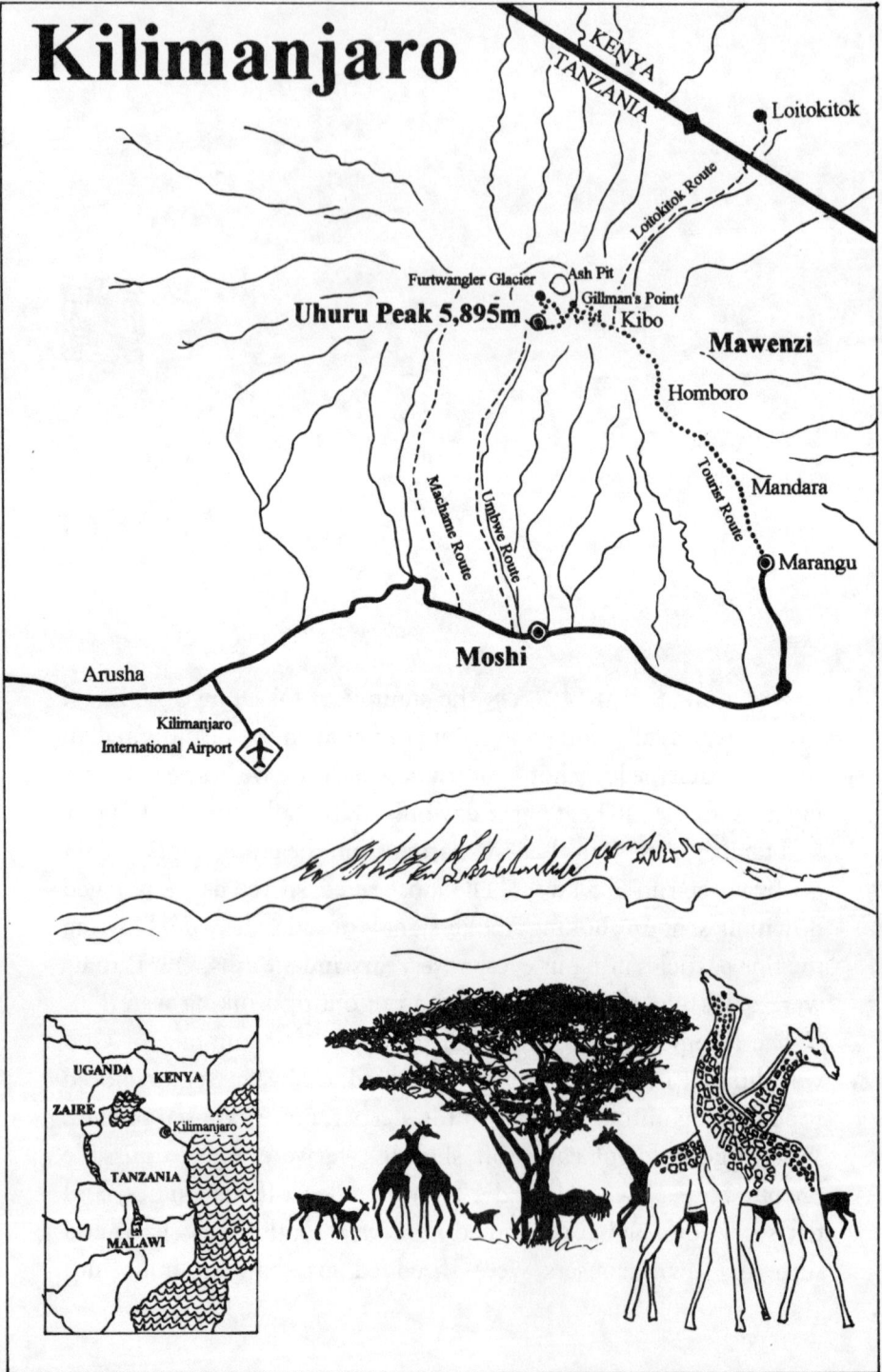

Kilimanjaro

KENYA
TANZANIA

Loitokitok

Loitokitok Route

Furtwangler Glacier
Ash Pit
Gillman's Point

Uhuru Peak 5,895m
Kibo

Mawenzi

Homboro

Mandara

Machame Route

Umbwe Route

Tourist Route

Marangu

Moshi

Arusha

Kilimanjaro
International Airport

UGANDA
KENYA
ZAIRE
Kilimanjaro
TANZANIA
MALAWI

the descent, I shuddered to think what damage was being wreaked where direct contact with flesh prevailed. Those lovely lustrous buttocks I'd eyed for the entire ascent were surely being scarred for life ...

Wherever it was possible to stand without toppling over, we tried balancing in the pose of surfboard riders and let the constantly shifting scree take us for a slow, wild ride. It was exhausting—not exhilarating—work, and what with the devilish heat and fatigue it soon became obvious the mountain, unlike any other I knew, was going to take as long to descend as it did to climb.

Halfway down it seemed as if the trail would never end. Paul's car was still just a tiny sequin in the folded cape of yellowed tussock wrapped around the base of the volcano. Our thirst became an all-consuming concern.

Two hours became three and every muscle ached. Three hours became four, and the only thing that kept us going was knowing that we'd left a flask of water back at the car.

Chris and I were almost delirious when we reached the vehicle. Our tongues were swollen and we could barely talk. Paul was prone in the narrow shadow of its back wheels. He could scarcely manage a wave. He pointed to the water bottle on the back seat of the car, but when I picked it up my heart sank. It was completely empty.

Phillip, the camp manager we'd hired to guard the car and its contents, had not only found and drunk the water, he'd pinched our lunch from the glove box as well. Paul had already used the last of his energy telling him off, but just in case he didn't quite get the message, Chris let loose with a barrage of abuse as well.

Phillip was cringing half-beneath the steering wheel, apologising for his thoughtlessness and begging not to be abandoned in the fearful wilderness. Chris reckoned he should walk the 30 kilometres to his camp, but eventually we decided two wrongs didn't make a right and reduced his sentence to a pay cut. He was lucky to be getting anything at all and he knew it.

The whole way back he grovelled and begged and apologised until we all screamed at him to 'just shut the fuck up!' Paul drove like a bat out of hades, the attendant breeze cooling us off a little, but nothing would soothe or placate us until we reached water.

We hit the camp, checked our tent, then staggered down to the river, tumbling from a cleft in the escarpment wall below the Serengeti. It was full of soda, but taste was hardly an issue; we drank as if there was no tomorrow. Paul and Chris submerged themselves in the comparatively icy flow, but an audience had quickly formed and its presence prevented me from joining them.

Phillip woke us the next morning, keen to erase the blot on his copybook as early as possible. I struggled out of the tent, put a pot on the stove for tea and called the boys from their body bags. I was stiff all over, every inch of my body begging for mercy, but thankfully my lungs had held up under the somewhat premature strain. Chris couldn't move at all and Paul was only marginally more agile for the Le Enkai experience.

Our illustrious camp manager had drawn a little mud-map for us, detailing an alternative route out of the region and back to the foot of Kilimanjaro. Instead of retracing our tracks through the Avenue of Volcanoes and its barren terrain, we could drive up onto the edge of the vast Serengeti, follow its boundary around to the southern gate, head on to Ngorongoro Crater National Park, complete the loop at Mto Wa Mbu and cruise on the 104 down to 'Kili'. We all agreed it was the perfect option and Phillip assured us his distances were not 'guesstimates' but factualities. If we were worried about petrol, we could detour at the top of the Serengeti escarpment and head further north to the little Maasai township of Wasso. Had it not been for the international border, we could have dropped in on Catherine and Robert while we were at it!

Paul was getting a tad stressed about time—he wanted to spend a few of his days off in Nairobi with Susan and their wee baby, Leena. It would take at least two days to return to Kilimanjaro by the circuit route and another to get back to the Kenyan capital, which effectively meant we'd have to bypass a few of the touristy destinations along the way. We would have to forgo some of Tanzania's premier safari locations such as Lake Manyara and Olduvai Gorge—the celebrated 'cradle of mankind'.

We consoled ourselves with a planned stopover at Ngorongoro, and with that destination in mind for the day we quickly set about dismantling our camp.

Wandering over to open the car, I noticed the back right tyre was completely flat. We had a spare, of course, but if we scored another puncture on the wild and rocky roads skirting the Serengeti, we'd be up the creek without a paddle. One could wait for days for another vehicle to pass; the route we'd be taking was well away from the regular tourist beat and only occasionally frequented by locals. Phillip referred to it as a 'highway', but we knew the best we could hope for was a barely visible set of wheel ruts.

We changed tyres, loaded up the car, jumped aboard and headed off towards Lake Natron. So far so good. The road was strewn with petrol-tank-and-chassis-cracking boulders, but most of them were avoidable. Poor Chris was in for a bad time, given the state of Paul's shock absorbers and lack of head room in the rear of the car, but he resigned himself to suffer in silence.

We started on the 'road of 17 turns', zigzagging our way up the escarpment wall. Strange stunted boabs were all the rocky ground could support here, each trifid-like tentacle bearing a single exquisite pink bloom. We stopped a few times to fossick, as Paul was even more obsessed by gemstones than Chris. Actually, his knowledge of rocks was quite extensive and Chris learnt a great deal from watching where and how he looked for possible 'specimens'.

We reached the top of the escarpment, checked the petrol gauge and headed south. At first the road was reasonably distinct, but 40 kilometres along it petered out to nothing. We were in the middle of the ultimate 'notorious nowhere', with not a blade of grass or shrub in sight, nothing but dead flat empty zilch, stretching out in every direction. It was completely devastated—and devastating to behold.

According to Phillip's 'factualities', we should have reached the main trans-Serengeti road by now, but there was nothing out there to indicate we were even remotely close. The only 'highway' we could see comprised the hoof-worn trails of the migratory route. Our thoughts were suddenly weighted by a nagging sense of *déjà vu*.

We all felt we must have missed a turn-off somewhere. We had no choice but to backtrack, thereby using up more fuel than we had anticipated and possibly necessitating a trip to Wasso. Disappointed, Paul turned the car around and started heading back.

After about 10 kilometres, another vehicle appeared—a dilapidated Land Rover crammed with a dozen Arusha-bound locals from Wasso and its neighbouring township of Loliondo. We flagged it down, and through one of the passengers who spoke English learned we *were* on the right track. It was just Phillip's sense of distance, not direction, that had thrown the journey into a spin.

The English-speaking passenger offered to travel with us to ensure we made it across the Serengeti wasteland. The vehicular tracks were less distinct the further one ventured, and without a suitable map and compass, experience was called for. He swapped places with Chris, and the driver of the local 'bus' agreed to travel in tandem, lest we run out of petrol along the way. We still had several hundred kilometres to go, not 50-odd.

By the time we reached the Ngorongoro Conservation Area headquarters, the petrol tank was bone-dry. The last five kilometres we travelled on faith and fumes: the 40-litre petrol tank actually took 41 litres of fuel on board at the Ngorongoro service station. We couldn't believe our luck; no further flat tyres either! We paid US$9 (the preferred currency in these parts) to have the puncture repaired, but like any workmanship in Tanzania, it was a pretty slap-dash and shoddy mend and consequently deflated overnight.

We camped on the rim of Ngorongoro, the largest unflooded caldera on earth. Officially gazetted as a World Heritage Site, Ngorongoro was a universally acclaimed natural wonder of the world. We stood on the very edge of the campground at sunset and looked down into the wide, flat-floored bowl of the extinct volcanic crater, but the perspective was not forthcoming. We were too far away to see any of the supposedly abundant wildlife and drought had robbed the vista of much of its colour. So much for the celebrated 'Garden of Eden'. From where we were, it looked disappointingly bleak.

Nothing, of course, could have been further from the truth. A drive down into the crater early the next morning revealed Ngorongoro for what it was: a truly rare phenomenon, more grandiose, more superlative than even the most verbose guidebook or brochure description promised. It was undeniably wondrous.

We descended through a ring of storm clouds, brooding all around the orbital rim of the crater. Below, dead-centre, the lens of its soda lake was covered with a cataract of low-lying mist. When the rising sun broke through the thinner clouds above, its rays formed lashes of light across the fragile grassy lids encircling the iris of the caldera. The haze dissipated. The whole landscape blinked; the right eye of the earth opened, as if the kiss of sunshine were breaking it free from a sleeping spell. The beauty it beheld was transcendent.

There were so many different types of habitats held within the confined 20-kilometre-wide crater floor: open grass plains, forests of fever-tree, swamplands and marshes, reed-sheltered ponds— each environment a world unto itself. We drove through and past them all, gazing out in sheer disbelief at 25 000 zebra, gazelle and wildebeest, stopping to watch a lion service his personal harem, peeping through binoculars, like voyeurs, at a family of hippos wallowing in the muddy waters of a secluded pool.

We spent several hours in rapture; it was the safari experience to rival all others on the continent, and seeing it was something I shall never forget as long as I live. How magnificent Africa must have been when such paradise was the rule, not the exception!

As we drove away from the open air gallery of wildlife I took back everything I'd ever said in the negative about spotting animals from a car. It was the only viable, responsible and safe way Ngorongoro custodians could deal with the *en masse* tourism such a unique site compelled. The humans had been caged, not the wildlife, and both were better off for the switch. I couldn't seem to get my lower jaw up. It was stuck, as it had been all morning, agape.

My mind was full of the images it had recorded inside the crater and as we sped towards and through Arusha, I could think of little else. Only when Kilimanjaro loomed into view was I jolted from my zoological reverie.

I couldn't believe it at first; it was so *huge*. I knew it was the largest free-standing mountain on the face of the earth and I had seen countless photographs of it before, but no amount of fore-warning prepared me adequately for what was very quickly filling the frame of Paul's windscreen. It was just enormous.

It rose from the flat, dry plains of northern Tanzania without warning. There were no foothills to blunt its urgency; its snow-cap was as incongruous when glimpsed through a heat haze and swirling columns of fine desert dust as it must have seemed the day it was 'discovered' almost a century and a half ago. It was easy to see why John Rebmann, the German-born missionary acredited as the first European to behold it, was rebuffed by the Royal Geographical Society in London when he claimed he'd seen ice on the equatorial giant. Now, 145 years later, with the monolith directly in front of me, I was still having trouble believing its existence.

Of course the Chagga[1] people, who had lived for aeons on the mountain's fertile southern slopes, knew of its shining summit long before any white man even set foot on the continent, but it was not in their nature to presume its discovery, or question what they deemed a sacred realm. In the years preceding Rebmann's visit, their efforts to reach the top of their mountain homeland had failed, giving rise to fabulous legends and frightful stories of the conditions and experiences encountered *en route*. Like so many mountains the world over, Kilimanjaro's apex was believed to be occupied by supernatural beings, who in this case were said to guard great hoards of gold, silver and precious stones. Any mere mortal who dared trespass upon it would surely die for his audacity.

The mountain continued to repel all who tried to climb it for a further 41 years. The Germans, inspired rather than bemused by Rebmann's claims, mounted numerous expeditions to conquer the peak, linking them more with the mountain's history than any other European interest. Professor Hans Meyer, a Leipzig geographer, and Ludwig Purtscheller, a distinguished German alpinist of the day, finally reached the top of Kibo—the highest of the three peaks which actually comprise Kilimanjaro—on 6 October, 1889.

Kilimanjaro was no longer a solely German obsession: these days people from all nations, all walks of life and all age and size groups came to Tanzania determined to complete an ascent. It was the dream of every traveller on the continent to stand on the rooftop of Africa.

Today there is a well-worn 'tourist route' up the side of the immense mountain, but its summit still remains unattainable to most. Fewer than 30 per cent of the 8–10 000 people who attempt the climb annually succeed in reaching the 5895-metre summit, now called Uhuru[2] Peak.

---

[1] One of the largest of Tanzania's 120 tribal groups.
[2] Swahili word for freedom.

When Chris and I finally ventured to the Kilimanjaro National Park gate at Marangu, the starting point for any summit-bound party, we were amazed at not only the number of would-be climbers *queuing* to pay the mandatory entrance and hut fees, but the physical composition of the throng as well.

With Paul safely on his way back to Nairobi, we were destined to share our trail with not one, but several dozen colourful characters. There were retired German couples in baggy shorts and long socks, frail middle-aged Japanese women wearing serious frowns, white gloves and terry-towelling hats, a couple of blond-haired blue-eyed Swedes in tailored designer-label denim, a husband and wife team from Beverly Hills wearing matching camouflage jackets, two Texans in ten-gallon hats—yes, even a token Aussie dressed to kill in a pair of Stubbies and thongs.

In keeping with the cosmopolitan flavour of the mountain, all payments were being made in American dollars or foreign-currency traveller's cheques. Tanzanian shillings were unacceptable tender. Needless to say, the cost of climbing the mountain rivalled its altitude.

We had made arrangements to hire a crew of four porters and a guide through an affable Kilimanjaro tour operator named Minja. It seemed an excessively large number of staff for just two people, especially since we were going to be pretty well looking after ourselves on the mountain, but Minja assured us it wasn't so much a case of overkill as insurance. The team he'd selected worked well together, and where Chaggas were concerned, it was always a case of 'the more the merrier'.

Their wages were actually the cheapest component of the whole venture, so we weren't about to deny any of them the chance to earn a slice of the great greenback pie. Besides, they were all assembled and ready to go by the time we'd completed the necessary paperwork and obtained our official receipts.

The Kilimanjaro National Park headquarters were made up of

a neat row of sturdy wooden A-frame chalets, surprisingly well finished and maintained. It was a far cry from the similarly functional reed and timber outpost built at the entrance to the Saharan Ahaggar, or the canvas tent pitched at the foot of Uganda's Ruwenzoris.

The complex, like the other hut-cities which were supposedly situated along the regimentedly organised Tourist Route, had been built with Norwegian aid money and assistance, which made me wonder where the government had siphoned all the foreign exchange the park previously earned. They were charging the highest daily entrance and camping fees of any national park in the world, amassing millions in annual revenue, but clearly little was being spent on improving the infrastructure of the tourism industry the mountain spawned. None had been spent on the roadway leading up to Kilimanjaro, or any other Tanzanian park, for that matter: they were all (at best) atrocious. The huts on Kilimanjaro's main tourist route were the only ones which were properly maintained—others, such as those on the next most popular Machame route were completely out of repair, but renovating them was not something the National Park Authority would likely consider until a well-meaning foreign government provided additional cash to pay for it.

Once again, I seemed to be the only one worrying about such matters. The other tourists were signing over fistfuls of traveller's cheques without a second thought for where the money would end up.

If one issue alone riled me more than any other, it was Africa's almost total lack of accountability. It was the main reason why the continent was financially as leaky as the proverbial sieve and why the majority always suffered while the select few prospered. Project-funding by the IMF was not always liable or dependent on completion agreements, so governments were pretty well free to pilfer as much money as they dared. Foreign aid was regularly

siphoned into off-shore bank accounts and food aid only served
to liberate governments further from their fundamental respon-
sibilities. Instead of using public funds to feed their people, they
were able to spend it on themselves, their personal whims and
their armies.

Few African nations were free of such corruption; indeed it was
endemic. In 1986 Liberia was forced into bankruptcy because of
unrestrained government spending, venality and the squandering
of US$375 million in aid. During the 1984 famine crisis in
Ethiopia, Mengitsu blew US$100 million celebrating the 10th
anniversary of his 'socialist revolution'. With callous indifference
to the plight of the nation's ordinary people, some US$10 million
worth of scotch whisky was airlifted into Addis Ababa for the
festivities. Bokassa, the former ruler of the Central African
Republic, spent millions of aid dollars on self-glorifying shows—
he declared and crowned himself emperor in 1977 and the French
government of the day picked up the US$20-odd million tab. It
was thought that over 3000 Nigerians have Swiss bank accounts
and that Kenya's elite have hoarded billions of dollars abroad—
possibly more than their country's entire foreign debt. Secret files
of the IMF and World Bank were reputedly full of reports on
corruption at the top in Zaire and suffering at the bottom; while
the nation's transportation network, agriculture and basic industries decline and crumble, Mobutu, the President, has amassed an
estimated personal fortune of $5 billion.

In most cases, the predominantly rural local populations were
powerless to do anything about the injustices their governments
and heads of state meted out to them. They had accustomed themselves to hunger, lack of education, unemployment and poor
health; illiteracy kept the majority ignorant of national affairs and
fear of retribution silenced those privy to the scam.

When you can't beat the system, you join it; further up the
social ladder, civil servants—taking advantage of bureaucratic
and administrative opportunities—lined their pockets with bribes.

Throughout Africa, smuggling, theft, usury, embezzlement, extortion, middleman activity and speculation were often as important income sources for urban families as formal employment. Low and irregularly paid salaries forced customs officers, police, social-service workers—even teachers and nurses—into demanding private payments for the performance of public services.

Before I had a chance to ask the Kilimanjaro staffers any impertinent questions about the eventual destination of their daily wad of foreign exchange, Chris had me gagged and hog-tied with our climbing rope. Ever the tactful one, he gently steered me away from the registration desk and dragged me up to the entrance gate.

Our porters were there, weighing up their loads and rearing to go, but our mandatory guide, Mathias, was nowhere to be seen. Minja assured us he'd come along in due course, but we didn't see the guy for another three days.

As soon as we set foot on the trail, I stopped raving about the need for freedom of speech and subsequent accountability of government spending. The forest creeping up the lower flank of the mountain was unexpectedly beautiful, and my attentions were quickly distracted.

For expediency's sake, most tourists trekked along the dirt road which led from the park gate to a point just half an hour shy of the first collection of bungalows at Mandara. Just by chance Chris and I had asked Minja if there was an alternative route, and on his instructions our porters led the way through a series of banana plantations and Chagga shambas (or gardens), and onto a little used pathway.

There was nothing better than having one's expectations surpassed. Everything I'd read about 'The Tourist Route' suggested it was the least attractive of the six Kilimanjaro tracks, a veritable four-lane highway lined with discarded tissues and sweet wrappers. We had chosen to take it only because it was the cheapest option, and we were on a tight budget. We planned to 'splurge' what we saved on an overnight stay inside the dormant crater, something very few people had done before, but according to Clive Ward—the man who'd taken us up Mount Kenya—the ultimate Kilimanjaro experience.

So here we were, fully prepared for disappointment, suddenly entering a lush, enchanted forest. Huge camphor, buttressed yellowwood and massive fig trees towered overhead, orchids and moss festooning their boughs. Secret steep-sided ravines, hidden in the shadows, were padded with delicate ferns and palms.

There was very little undergrowth; it was regularly scythed by the Chagga women from surrounding shambas. Dozens of them were on the trail returning from their latest 'harvest', the fruits of their labour compacted into two-metre long 'bricks' of succulent cattle fodder.

As we moved further and higher into the forest, wispy beards of Spanish moss began to appear in the trees, adding their own special magic to the scene. The earth smelled rich and pure.

Our porters walked heal to toe, balancing their loads on top of their heads, as opposed to carrying them on their backs. They were young fellas, working hard to support their families, and one of them—a baby-faced 20-year-old named Happy God—was studying English part-time with the view to one day becoming a guide. His father was the caretaker at the top hut on the mountain, and Chris and I mused how appropriate his own first name seemed in lieu of his position: Happy God's dad had been christened Good Luck.

The huts at Mandara were amazing. They had porcelain flushing loos, a dining hall and two dozen 8-bed A-frame sleeping chalets outfitted with solar lighting, mattresses and pillows! We could scarcely believe we were on a mountain, and not checking into some luxury ski resort. I've never spent any time at all in the European Alps, but I imagined the accommodation was comparable.

The next day we trekked through the last and steepest section of the rain forest, then meandered through a glade of giant heather and tussock grass. Higher up, closer to Homboro—the second 'tourist village' on the route—those plants became more stunted and the first lobelias and groundsels appeared.

The number of people moving to and fro along the trail was absolutely daunting. Half of those descending looked as if they'd been to hell and back and none of them offered any encouragement whatsoever to those ascending. In fact, both groups largely ignored each other. Chris and I did our damnedest to be civil and got the occasional acknowledgment for our efforts, but by and large it was the unfriendliest atmosphere I'd ever encountered on a mountain. People going up were preoccupied by doubt and dread, people coming down were consumed by failure and exhaustion.

Many tourists under-estimated Kilimanjaro and the effect its high altitude could have on the human body. Unfortuately the standard five-day trip the tour companies and National Parks Authority promoted was not sufficiently long enough for most people to acclimatise. Their primary concern was not for client comfort or success, but for commerce; the faster they could get people up and down the mountain, the more people they could push through the turnstiles.

Homboro huts were situated at 3700 metres and many of our trail comrades arrived there feeling off-colour. Ignoring the early warning signs of altitude-related illness, they were going to let determination get in the way of commonsense and deny their bodies a chance to 'catch up'. At least half the people in the main dining hut that afternoon were picking disinterestedly at their food and complaining of headaches, but all of them were talking of pushing on up to Kibo, the top hut, next day. Chris and I shuddered to think of the potential disaster in store; even if some of them made it to Uhuru Peak, they'd be in no fit state to enjoy the experience. The upper trail through the scree which led to the crater rim of Kili was supposedly lined with vomit and empty bubble-packs of Panadol . . .

I was feeling great, which at 3700 metres meant my lungs must have fully recovered from their wee bout of pneumonia. Chris had a bit of a stomach upset, which could mean only one thing: we were about to run into Doctor Patricia and the elephant man again. Sure enough, they pulled into Homboro just on dark, having summited that morning via the Machame Route.

They both looked shattered; completely drained by the climb. Despite their relatively fit state and previous altitude conditioning on Mount Kenya, Kilimanjaro had nonetheless wreaked a generous share of havock on our friends. Chris and I consequently descided to not only take a day off at Homboro, but one at Kibo hut as well—there was no way we were going to pay all that money and come all that way and not live to tell a happy tale of adventure. It was high time a written account of the climb was actually positive in outlook!

Our day off at Homboro was spent making a side-trip up to the base of Mawenzi, the more significant of Kilimanjaro's 'other' two peaks. It was a mountain in its own right; a craggy old castle completely different in character and form to Kibo. According to Chagga legend, when the two old volcanoes were still 'smoking their pipes', Mawenzi's was somehow extinguished. He went to his bigger but younger brother Kibo to borrow fire, but a short time later (after taking a nap) his pipe went out for a second time. Mawenzi returned to ask Kibo for another light, but the younger brother became very angry and thrashed him savagely with a club.

The Chagga believe that Mawenzi was so ashamed of his subsequent appearance, he tried to hide his battered and broken face behind clouds as often as he could. Indeed as Chris and I approached the poor old clobbered peak, high horsetails whipped around the summit spires. By the time we reached the base camp, the entire top half of the mountain was enveloped in cloud.

We ate lunch, then hot-footed it back to the hut at Homboro. Bob and Senia, our two sun-worshipping room-mates, whom we'd earlier convinced to take the day off, had redressed and buried themselves in down, teasing each other with true confessions and tall tales. Chris and I joined in and before long our four-bunked hut was rocking with laughter.

Senia was an air hostess with Delta Airlines in real life, and Bob was a teacher turned attorney. Collectively, our repetoire of jokes lasted well into the night and resumed as soon as the sun rose the following day. There was no stopping any of us; we were determined to have a good time on the legendary mountain of misery and set out for Kibo in excellent spirits.

Mathias, who had finally appeared on the scene the afternoon before, fell into step with Chris and me immediately. He was a lovely, gentle man, full of humour and charming stories. When we reached the vast barren saddle which separated Kibo from Mawenzi and Kenya from Tanzania, the wind threatened to blast us back to Horombo. It was strong enough to lean on and colder than an arctic gale.

A blanket of low-lying cloud spread as far as the eye could see from just below the northern side of the saddle right across Kenya. Mathias laughed when he saw it, for it wasn't the first time he'd seen such a spectacle. 'When I was a boy,' he reminisced, casting his gaze across the unbroken white landscape of cloud, 'before they invented school, I used to think this was the end of the world.' I searched all around, but I couldn't find a discarded Coke bottle anywhere.

The day's quota of summit hopefuls were making their return to Homboro. Some were being carried by friends, two were on bicycle-wheeled stretchers, all but three had failed and every single one of them was pale beyond belief. The successful trio didn't exactly glow with their achievement, but at least they were walking upright and capable of weak smiles.

Senia had a slight headache when we reached Kibo hut, a five-roomed dormitory-style concrete block at 4703 metres. Chris, Bob and I felt great. It was nearly as cold inside the building as out, but tourists were arriving in a steady stream, slowly warming the air. As for the atmosphere, it remained decidedly frigid. Most of the overnight inmates felt lousy and several went so far as to ask those of us in finer fettle to quell our mirth.

They all went to bed early, with little or no dinner, but sleep escaped most of them and nausea kept several struggling back and forth from the long-drop toilet.

At midnight everyone who was going to attempt to climb the mountain freed themselves from their sleeping bags and readied their chosen battledress for the ocassion. Their dutiful guides brought them tea and sweet glucose biscuits, but most found it hard to keep food down. Chris and I got up to farewell Bob and Senia, then crawled back into our warm cocoons for a few more hours' sleep.

As soon as the last stragglers left the hut, the first of those defeated by cold, exhaustion and illness returned. Their disappointment was obvious. Chris and I tried to console those who came back into our own room, but tears welled in saddened eyes and voices broke with the weight of self-failure. Some holiday this turned out to be.

Senia reappeared just after sunrise. Her headache had worsened and she'd decided to turn back while she was still able to do so under her own steam. Commonsense prevailed over ambition, and at least she knew she'd given it her best shot and therefore had nothing further to prove.

Kilimanjaro brought out the best and the worst sides of human aspiration and ignored everything else in between. Climbing it was an 'all or nothing' affair for just about everyone who chose to accept its challenge and few would be content to leave without ultimate success. Reaching Gillman's Point—a landmark on the actual rim of the crater but 3.5 horizontal kilometres and a little under 200 vertical metres short of the summit beacon—was a fantastic achievement in its own right, but many of those who made it there and no further felt they had little to celebrate.

Chris and I eventually left the hut at 8.30am and wandered up to Hans Meyer Cave, a rock overhang halfway up the sliding scree slope leading towards the top of Kili. By the time we got there, the people who had battled the elements, conquered self-doubt and pushed themselves onward and upward to the summit were making their way back to Kibo. Some were racing down the scree, others were literally crawling and a few were being carried by their guides. All of them confessed to being completely dehydrated. If this were the Himalaya—a little further from the Equator where the air at comparable altitudes was noticeably thinner—half of them would have been dead.

Chris rolled tape and we videoed our mate Bob descending. He was suddenly overcome with emotion and exhaustion and burst into tears and laughter at the same time. He had never driven his physical self so hard or so far, and doing so clearly meant more to him than he was able to express in words. He could not describe the view from the summit, only the feelings he had on reaching it. He'd have to wait for the photographs he took from the top to be processed in order to remember the mountain's more corporeal perspectives.

These were many, as Chris and I were soon to find out over the following two days. The last thing on earth we wanted to confront was a midnight start, so that evening we asked Mathias not to wake us until the first hint of morning lightened the horizon. Midnight came and went, and with it 40 of the 50 tourists who'd replaced the previous day's throng headed cheerlessly up the mountain.

We waited until sunrise, ate a big breakfast then started out right on 6.30am. It was the most glorious day, completely windless and for the moment cloudless. Just before Gillman's we came upon one of the larger ascending groups that had left Kibo in the wee small hours. They were totally shattered and, unbelievably, still on their way up, not down, the mountain. It was 9.45am. I wasn't sure whether their determination was admirable or suicidal, but to a person they were completely speechless. When

Chris and I bounded past it must have been totally demoralising.

There was nothing superhuman about our fortitude or strength; we'd just spent a couple of days longer on the mountain than most people, and as such were better acclimatised and equipped for the summit experience.

We hit the rim and drooled over the snow-covered scape which filled much of the massive caldera of Kilimanjaro. We couldn't see the ash pit itself from Gillman's Point, nor the Furtwangler Glacier where we hoped to make camp, but the distant Northern Icefields were resplendent in the sun. Behind them, cloud was starting to rise up from Kenya and within the hour we were swamped—sitting on the summit waiting for random glimpses of Africa from Uhuru.

Chris and I danced around up there for a while, and I copied down the inspiring, optimistic words etched in a plaque which crowned the summit. They were taken from a speech Julius Nyerere delivered at the time of independence and invoked Kilimanjaro as a metaphor for his nation's aspirations. The quote was as poignant today as it was in 1961, its message made all the more relevant on a global scale because of the variety and diversity of people who would read it for the first time in this most sacrosanct surrounding. 'We the people of Tanganyika,'[3] it read, 'would like to light a candle and put it on top of Mount Kilimanjaro, which would shine beyond our borders giving hope where there was despair, love where there was hate and dignity where before there was only humiliation.'

I prayed that such idealism still had a place in Africa's heart and more of a role to play in the shaping of its future.

After an hour, we descended into the great sweeping maw of Kilimanjaro. Much of the floor of the crater was covered in nieve penitenetes—a formation peculiar to snowfields at high altitudes where radiation and atmospheric conditions combine to turn the

---

[3] Tanganyika united with Zanzibar to form the United Republic of Tanzania in 1964.

fall into a wonderland garden of glistening stalagmites. You couldn't actually walk across such a surface; you had to kick your way through it, and that was pretty tiring work at an altitude of 5000 metres.

We reached a small island—a mound of snow-free frozen earth— and decided to call it quits. It was as good a site as any for a camp and we had the tent up in no time. Happy God had come up with the rest of our camping gear and we melted some snow to share a cuppa with him before he descended to Kibo. Mathias had a half-reasonable sleeping bag and no qualms whatsoever about staying the night inside the crater; 50 greenbacks went a long way towards ensuring his companionship—as did the promise of a three-course gourmet packet meal.

The management and staff at the Arcadia Twin Cinema back home in Ulladulla had given Chris and me a present just before we left town in April, destined for the great Sahara. We had vowed not to open it until we were on the top of Kilimanjaro itself, but everyone assumed we'd weaken and consume the contents on the drive up to Sydney. I won't deny that we wanted to do just that—at least a dozen times actually—but somehow we resisted the temptation and opened the gift on the roof of Africa, as promised. It was a box of liqueur chocolates, and even though the use-by date was up, they were delicious with our coffee, a fitting treat for the end of another marvellous climb.

We were a long way from the crowded huts on the Tourist Route; a thousand kilometres from the whingeing, retching, snoring masses. Hundreds of Lilliputian people were crawling over the giant sleeping body of Kilimanjaro, but here in the very centre of its heart, we were completely alone. At last. The serenity was holy.

The clouds dispersed and the Furtwangler Glacier shone like molten gold in the sunset. It was a massive wave, suspended in time like a photograph, taking all the dreams of the world towards some unknown shore. It was a tapestry, a rich brocade of liquid thread and the lustrous hair of angels.

The sea of snow crystal penitenetes shone, and not one but ten thousand candles were suddenly aflame. Nyerere's dream of peace was whispering on the breeze.

The whole crater was so silent, so divine, as close to heaven as a prayer. There we were, nestled in the very palm of God; sheltered from the troubled world, believing life was perfect.

HIGH IN THE
ETHIOPIAN SIMIENS

T HE EXPEDITION WAS slowly drawing to a close. All up, we had about seven weeks to go: one to get off the mountain and back to Nairobi, another to log our Tanzanian journey and prepare for the three weeks we anticipated spending in the Simien Mountains of Ethiopia, one to fly to and climb Mount Cameroon in the west and, depending on flight schedules, one to shop, party and head on home.

We scored a ride back to Kenya in a DHL courier van which doubled as the international bus service between Moshi and Nairobi. It was great to catch up on all the news and gossip we'd missed, and the second of our countdown weeks flew by in a blur. Like Australians all over the world, our diplomatic buddies from the High Commission were still celebrating Sydney's success in winning the Olympics bid for 2000.

Clive Ward, the spindly safari guide we'd trekked with on Mount Kenya, was as keen as mustard to join Chris and me in

Ethiopia

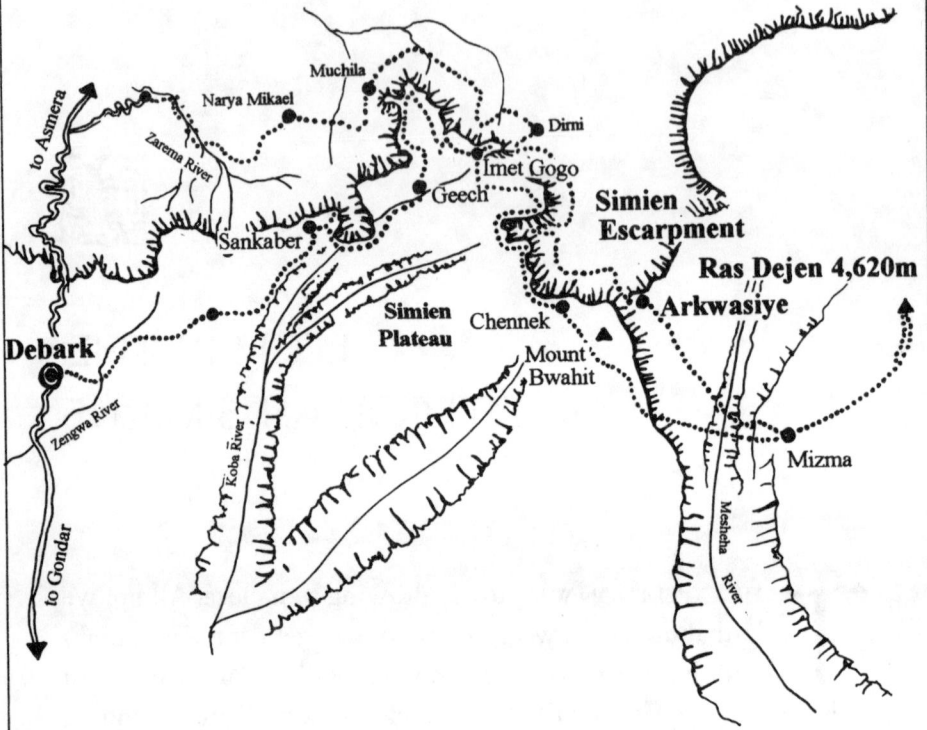

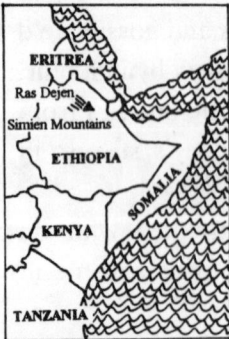

Ethiopia, so we met a few times to formulate some basic plans over a beer or two. Unfortunately Clive's favourite watering hole was 'Buffalo Bill's', a well-known girlie-bar frequented by white expatriates and tourists ripe for a bit of post-safari cultural exchange.

Most first-time male visitors were embarrassing to watch. They were like little kids let loose in Time Zone—only their pockets bulged with condoms, not coins, and black women lined the walls instead of slot machines. The way some blokes treated the prostitutes suggested they didn't know the difference, playing with their tits as if they were flipper controls and kicking when they realised they'd lost their last ball. It would have been amusing, if it weren't so degrading.

Anything can and did happen at Buffalo Bill's and five minutes in the women's toilet completely stripped me bare of innocence. The tiny convenience was the lair of the pub lionesses: part-drug den, part-smoking lounge, part-clothing store, part-change room, part-sick bay, part-boxing ring ('He's mine, OK? I saw him first. You keep your hands off him!'), part-beauty salon, part club-house—which wasn't bad considering the total area was little more than two metres square. I went in for a pee and I came out with a complete education.

Somehow, in the extraordinarily noisy confusion of the public bar, we managed to nut out the logistics of our Simien journey and on 7 October, the three of us boarded a plane bound for the Ethiopian capital, Addis Ababa. We missed our connecting flight up to the northern township of Gondar, but the airline had arranged an unscheduled trip in an old Twin Otter to clear a backlog of passengers, and we were able to get seats on it.

It was surprising how green and fertile Ethiopia looked from the air. I was part of the Western generation weaned, nurtured and matured on tragic images from the Horn of Africa, on pictures which catalogued a modern history of human suffering unequalled elsewhere on the globe. How could a place synonymous throughout my lifetime with drought, famine, war and oppression be so incredibly lush?

The entire area we flew over was chequered with luxuriant greens, each square bordered with rich black soil and dotted with a myriad of vivid yellow oilseed flowers. Cultivation went right up to the very edges of each highland plateau and tableland, and lined the wider valleys below. Improbably deep gorges and canyons were cut by rivers and fantastic isolated protrusions of rock stood boldly on the landscape like rows of carved chessmen.

We flew past the meandering course of the muddy Blue Nile and straight over its source, Lake Tana. In the afternoon light the huge water body glistened like an immense polished coin. The clouds overhead cast shadows across its silvery surface, forming fanciful portraits and profiles of past Ethiopian kings and queens.

It took the better part of twenty minutes to fly from the southern to northernmost shore, where we began our descent onto the dirt runway which serviced Gondar. Outside the simple arrival and departure hall at the airport we were besieged by taxi drivers vying for our fare to the city. A scuffle broke out when we followed a lean, well-dressed fellow by the name of Seyoum Yigzaw and tossed our luggage on the racks of what we assumed was his own badly dinged car. Words and punches were exchanged, and before we knew what was going down, we were speeding away from the scene as fast as we could.

Seyoum was not the driver we presumed him to be—just a tout, cleverer than most we'd met in Africa. He sat in the back seat with Chris and Clive and, unruffled by the shouts and abuse so recently hurled in his direction, began a running commentary on the history of Gondar. Like it or not, we'd been conned into hiring ourselves a 'private guide'.

You could hardly blame Seyoum for trying, but I chastised him anyway for the shameless way he'd solicited our business. I didn't want him to think we were stupid, or that his unscrupulous methods were acceptable to tourists and travellers the world over.

We Aussies were wise to most scams and did not generally appreciate being 'taken for a ride'. In fact, he was lucky we weren't throwing punches too.

Seyoum protested that he had a swag of references and that we were the only foreigners to voice such complaints—and he should know, because he'd hoodwinked nearly every newly arriving independent visitor since the resurgence of tourism in Gondar! He was doing us a favour actually; he was an expert in his field and his motivation was not profit-driven, but service-oriented. Of course, if we wanted to share a little of our rather obvious wealth with him in return for his advice and assistance he would be extremely grateful. How much? Oh, that was entirely up to us ... but please bear in mind the fact that he had a university degree and in all likelihood, he was worth much more than we would ever conceivably offer.

To be fair, Seyoum did have a glut of local knowledge, even if its delivery was as dry as an old textbook. He took himself terribly seriously and sincerely believed he was filling a need—succouring, not deceiving his country's foreign 'guests'. There was certainly a dearth of printed information on the various buildings and historically important sites around Gondar, so until the official government-run tourist office got its act together, Seyoum was guaranteed employment from suckers like us.

It was hard to believe Gondar, a relatively dilapidated township of just 95 000 souls, was once the second-largest city in the whole of Africa. For more than 200 years it had been the capital of Ethiopia—from the time King Fasiledes was crowned in 1632, to 1855, when it was despoiled of its treasures by the self-proclaimed emperor, Tewodros II. With Seyoum rattling off a well-remembered list of appropriate dates and regal-sounding names, we wound our way up one of several urban hillsides, past the ruins of half a dozen ancient churches and castles and entered the ramshackle city precincts.

We passed beneath a wide banner referring to more recent

events in the nation's history, which called for an end to political confusion and demanded a fair and safe democratic election. A second decried 'chauvinist oppression', but we were moving too quickly to read the name of the organisation so accused. What was poignant was not so much the sentiment or the situation prompting its expression as the realisation that freedom of speech had at last found its voice in Ethiopia, after more than 2000 years of nationhood.

We checked into a run-down, overgrown, almost empty hotel built by the Italians during their occupation of 1936–41. Inspired by Seyoum's initial history lesson, I unpacked a wad of photocopied notes I'd compiled back in Australia and settled back to read my way through them. I hadn't had the chance until now, and it suddenly seemed relevant to look them over.

Although Eritrea was colonised by Italy in 1890, Ethiopia as a whole remained independent and until the 1974 revolution, it was ruled by an unbroken succession of 225 emperors, each claiming descent from the celebrated union of King Solomon and the Queen of Sheba.

The last Emperor—Haile Selassie, King of Kings—introduced some modest reforms to the outmoded feudal system, but discontent was sweeping through his nation. Years of unease and resentment erupted and a series of strikes, riots and demonstrations led to military intervention, mutiny and a *coup d'état*. Selassie was deposed, the constitution suspended and the crown abolished in preparation for the establishment of a socialist republic. Lieutenant Colonel Mengistu Haile Mariam rose ruthlessly to become the chairman of the Provisional Military Administrative Council. He promised socialism and equality, but delivered war and economic stagnation.

Mengistu proved as autocratic as the old emperor, responding to a campaign waged in favour of civilian government over military rule by brutally killing those who dared oppose him. At his command, at least 10 000 'counter-revolutionaries' in Addis

Ababa were rounded up and shot. Relatives of some of those slain had to reimburse the authorities for the cost of the bullets before they could claim the bodies for burial.

At the same time this internal power struggle was taking place, the war against Eritrean secessionists, suspended by Selassie some fifteen years earlier, was in full swing up north. Somalia launched an invasion from the south east, and Ethiopia turned to the Soviet Union for help. Military spending increased from 25 to 50 per cent of the government budget. The USSR supported both wars with a billion dollars' worth of arms and ammunition per annum, further burdening the nation's debt and external dependence.

The combination of war and famine cost Ethiopia dearly in lives as well. The Eritrean war of independence left 100 000 Ethiopian soldiers, 50 000 Eritrean combatants and an unknown number of of civilians dead. During the famine of 1984–85 Mengistu put a higher priority on oiling his state machinery with foreign exchange than he did on feeding the hungry: while millions of Ethiopians starved to death, the government continued to export green beans to the UK. Mengistu partied on, squandering millions celebrating his 'Revolution' while another 100 000 Ethiopians died as a direct result of his forced 'resettlement' programs.

It took the people of Ethiopia 17 years to oust the Mengistu junta and install an interim government, substantially dominated by the Ethiopian People's Revolutionary Democratic Front. Over 60 political organisations emerged to contest leadership, greatly complicating the political process. For a moment in mid-1991, it looked as if the country was destined to resume its civil war. To add insult to injury, the worst drought of the century was continuing to affect much of Africa, and famine still threatened the lives of nearly eight million Ethiopians.

In contrast to the rest of Ethiopia, Eritrea had effectively become self-governing and appeared to be firmly under the control of the Eritrean People's Liberation Front. The longest war in Africa had finally come to an end and with vicious interclan warfare and banditry on the go in Somalia,[1] Eritrea was actually the most stable part of the Horn of Africa.

I was completely absorbed in my notes when Clive came to our room and suggested a stroll through town. With the help of Seyoum, we still had to organise some sort of transportation to Debark, a rural village which doubled as the gateway to the Simien Mountains National Park. Chris opted to stay behind and guard his video gear, since the door to our room wouldn't lock.

It was quite late in the afternoon before we managed to track down a vehicle with a safe amount of tread on the tyres and a relatively realistic rate of hire. The latter proved comparable to what we'd expect to pay for a taxi ride back home, but that was better than the 'limousine' quotes offered by the competition.

We were clearly on the wrong side of a 'supply and demand' situation: we agreed to pay one man an amount of money equal to the nation's per capita *annual* income for a journey of just one day's duration!

But what a journey it was, worth every last bir[2] of the fare. The landscape was even more stunning at ground level than it had been from the air. The condition of the road turned 105 kilometres into four of the most enjoyable hours I'd ever spent inside a car; we moved slowly enough to absorb just about every aspect of the scenery.

People looked up from the fields as we passed, waving and smiling and singing out a welcome. Children raced alongside the car as we crawled through the centre of village markets, squealing and pointing and screaming 'You! you! you!' until they ran out of breath. We stopped to buy some roasted cobs of corn in one shantytown, but we were mobbed in the process and forced to find lunch elsewhere. It was obviously still something of a novelty to see foreigners in these parts.

[1] By the end of 1992 an estimated 1.5 million people were thought to have perished from starvation and military action in Somalia.

[2] The Ethiopian unit of currency; the current exchange rate is approximately 5 Bir to the US dollar, or 3.5 to the Australian dollar.

As soon as we arrived in Debark we became the town's major attraction. You could tell from the way people pointed and looked and talked that they were watching and commenting on your every move and feature. I would have paid a king's ransom to have known what they were saying and thinking. Chris and I hadn't experienced anything like it for ages, since we'd ventured into the closed tribal state of Arunachal Pradesh in India, during our previous expedition across the Himalaya.

We checked into the local no-star hotel and paid off the taxi driver, then sought out and found the National Park headquarters, a corrugated tin and timber-lined office tucked out of sight on the main approach to town. The rooms were fairly spartan— a few tables, a pile of books, a map and several pages from a colourful brochure tacked to one wall. An antiquated radio set for communicating with the National Parks head office in Addis Ababa sat on a bench behind the empty desk of the chief warden.

We introduced ourselves to an attendant and asked if a guide named Getenet Akalu was available, or already out in the field. He came highly recommended by a group from the Mountain Club of Kenya who had previously undertaken a trek similar to the one we were planning and we were anxious to secure his services. The alternative sat on a bench in the warden's office, drunk out of his mind, talking in a babble of incomprehensible tongues and swaying like kid with a hoola-hoop.

We were in luck; a young boy was sent to find Getenet, and within half an hour we were shaking hands, grinning at each other and poring over the map on the wall.

We warmed to Getenet instantly. Radiating laughter lines puckered the skin around his small mischievous eyes and two prominent veins stood out on his forehead whenever he broadened his smile. He had a fuzzy crop of dark hair, a bumfluff moustache, a goatie beard and a wide-brimmed straw hat like a scarecrow. At a guess he was in his early forties, and since he only just passed my shoulder in height, I pegged him for 150 cm even.

There was a standard seven-day trek across the Simien plateau, but Getenet was happy to extend and stretch it anyway we chose and offered a few suggestions to help us firm up a plan. Chris and I had only one stipulation: that somehow the highest peak on the Horn of Africa—the 4620-metre Ras Dejen—be included in the route. It actually lay outside the boundary of the National Park, but a side trip to climb it would only use an additional two days. We wanted to spend at least two weeks exploring the region, so we searched the map for additional possibilities.

Getenet ran his finger along another trail which defined the northeastern boundary of the park. To the best of his knowledge, no post-revolution trekking parties had used it. A quick glance at the map was all we needed to agree—the route would give us quite a different perspective on the Simiens, as it switchbacked through the foothills below the great sheer cliff faces of the highlands.

Within the hour Getenet had the whole itinerary sorted out, the horsemen hired and two armed scouts booked for the journey. The area was once notorious for bandits and while the risk of an encounter was pretty minimal these days, old traditions died hard. It was still a mandatory park policy to travel under guard.

The main scout, like Getenet, was very good-looking, with fine-chiselled features and grey curly hair. The Ethiopians were very proud of their appearance, in particular their colour, accrediting God with its perfect manufacture. According to their traditional creation theory, God moulded men from clay. He put the first batch in the fire, but left them there too long and they came out burned and black. He threw them away down south. The second batch he took from the fire too soon, and they were pasty white. He threw them away to the north. The third lot came out just right, and of course they were placed in Ethiopia.

Getenet and the scouts spoke Amharic; Ethiopia's official tongue. They were devout members of the Ethiopian Orthodox Church, which practised an ancient form of Christianity based on the worship of the Ark of the Covenant. Seyoum later took us to an early morning mass in the Debre Berhan Selassie Church in Gondar, and for all the world it was hard to believe we were nearing the 21st Century. On entering the musty muralled vestibule we had somehow taken a giant leap backward in time. In the semi-darkness of the interior chamber a priest read from the bible in Ge'ez, an extinct spoken language from the 3rd or 4th century. A dozen white-robed deacons sang slow, solemn chants and beat a steady rhythm on drums. A flock of 300 angels stared down from the ceiling, each restored pair of eyes devoid of expression yet able to penetrate the soul.

We handed over the park fees and advanced half the sum of each man's wage to the attendant. Apparently the system was considered equitable, but I felt it was more to safeguard our interests, than those of the men we were temporarily employing. To make sure they didn't abandon us in the middle of the boonies, their money would remain in a safe until our journey was successfully completed and we reported back to the National Park office.

We gave Getenet a few hundred bir extra to purchase food and supplies for himself and crew, then walked back into town to the hotel. We were starving but the kitchen was closed and coffee was all they could offer until dinner. We killed time breaking down and repacking our kit into sack-sized bundles befitting for the horses, then at 6.30pm re-grouped in the dining hall.

Getenet ordered on our behalf, a fully traditional Ethiopian feast. Being a Friday, he was not permitted to eat meat, so we went completely vegetarian. Out came a massive basket of injera—sour, spongy, grey, fermented pancakes no less than a metre in diameter, made from three-day-old milk and wheat flour, covered in assorted odoriferous yet edible titbits.

Chris gave me one of his famous 'I hate it when you make me eat this shit' sort of looks, then tore off a small piece of the surprisingly soft and light injera, smothering it in taste-bud numbing chilli paste. I dipped my first piece in a curdled concoction of tart goat-milk yogurt and scooped up a lump of something that looked a little like overboiled spinach. Believe it or not, it was really quite delicious and by the end of the meal, having tried everything on offer, I was suitably impressed. Chris, who subscribed to the philosophy of 'never eat anything you can't at least describe', decided to suspend judgment until he got used to the totally different taste sensations. He was a meat and two veg lad from way back.

Clive, Getenet, Chris and I were up at 6.30 next morning, rearing to go. Our horsemen appeared an hour later and by 8.30am we were finally ready to leave the hotel. The Saturday market was just hotting up and people were arriving in droves from every conceivable direction. Those who were coming to sell or trade something had heavily laden donkeys by their sides, and those who were buying were as yet unencumbered. Nearly everyone was dressed in rags with a length of crude unbleached cloth (called a *shamma*) draped over his or her head, shoulders and upper torso. They were either bare-footed or wearing homemade sandals and many of the men carried wooden staffs and bottles to refill in the market with unrefined oil. Goats, sheep, horses and mules moved with each human caravan and the clip-clop of large hooves and patter of small filled the air with their music.

The whole scene was like something out of the Old Testament. It was a magnificent day—the sun was shining, the birds were singing, the landscape was tingling with joy. The trail ahead was clearly defined for another two hours by the stream of people who continued to flow across the highland from their distant villages towards Debark. Getenet knew many of them personally and paused to greet each one warmly.

We stopped for lunch at the home of one of the few Falasha families left in the Simien mountains. The region used to be something of a stronghold for the 'Black Jews of Ethiopia' who, despite threats of persecution, chose to remain faithful to Judaism after the conversion of the kingdom to Christianity in the 4th century. Further attempts to exterminate them took place in later centuries, but by the time Haile Selassie came to rule, conditions were improved: there were 19 000 Falashas in Ethiopia and their influence was growing.

But all that changed when Mengistu seized power and the Eritrean war got under way. The Israeli Government, fearing for the lives of their 'brethren', secretly airlifted more than 10 000 Falashas from their native country and resettled them in the Promised Land.

Getenet explained how the family we were now with had missed their chance to escape. Somehow they had managed to survive the ensuing persecutions and vagaries of war, but only by denying their faith to the authorities. Only in recent months had they felt safe enough to replace the Star of David on their roof, but financial constraints kept them from re-observing the Sabbath. The head of the household was the local knife-maker, and he was compelled to sell his wares at the Saturday market in Debark. To miss it would mean starving his family.

The Simiens had become something of a battleground during the civil war and while we swilled down our lunch with home-brew, served in polished cowhorn 'cups' plugged with wood, Getenet described what it was like to have lived through that time. Unlike too many of his friends, he and his family had escaped death at the hands of Mengistu's army—but not periodic interrogation, imprisonment and torture. Suspected of counter-revolutionary allegiances, Getenet had on several occasions been arrested and tortured on the soles of his feet with an electric cattle prod. To this day they still ached whenever he tried to walk barefoot, but it was nothing compared to past suffering. As he put it, 'Today even if a man has no job he is happy. He has peace; he can sleep nicely'. He closed his eyes and with his voice full of wonder he added, 'No sound of bombing ... no sound of gunfire ... no sound of aeroplane; it is very good now to be Getenet Akalu.'

The morning sky had gradually given way to afternoon clouds and by the time we were back on the trail to Sankaber, our camp-site for the evening, it was raining lightly and cold enough for a beanie and sweater. The highland was stunning, but even more beautiful were the children who roamed upon it with their family's livestock. Momentarily leaving their flocks and herds, they ran to greet us with huge open smiles. They placed their little lizard-like hands inside my own, their skin feeling so cold and scaly against the smooth warmth of my palm. Their eyes were as big as saucers, their twiggy bare legs as strong as forged steel. They all wore woollen hats they had spun and woven themselves and softened goathide capes around their shoulders. They looked so happy and healthy, so proud of who they were.

Curiosity drew me towards one small child carrying a baby sibling on her back. She had a fantastic, totally punk hairdo; her head had been shaved, save for a thin halo around the crown and two dissecting lines, like a cross on an easter bun, over the top of her skull. The baby's head was even more bizarre, for it had been forced into an elongated shape by the application of tight bandages for several months following birth. A well-shaped head was a source of great parental pride, but Getenet said the tradition of cranial swaddling had largely died out. Indeed, of all the babies we met in the highlands, we saw only three with their infant heads distorted.

It was just on dusk when we reached Sankaber and set up our camp amid the bombed ruins of a previous game warden's home. The site overlooked the lowland hills which, thanks to the cloud cover and low angle of the sun, appeared as tissue-thin layers of light. Each range was transparent, stretching away to the western horizon in subtle variegated shades of blue.

In the morning that same subdued scape was as solid as rock and I climbed up on the crumbling wall of the ruin to photograph the honey-pot hillocks below and the eroded crags and sheer bluffs lined up like dominoes far into the distance. They were amazing formations, like the steep-walled buttes of Arizona's Grand Canyon: not quite as barren, but equally spectacular.

After breakfast we packed up and trekked over to the edge of the precipitous cliff. The horsemen took a safer route with their charges, but Getenet and the scouts led us right along the edge of the abyss. I had never seen country like it before, with every step revealing a different unfolding tableau of views, and there was just no restraining my shutter-finger. Before I knew it, I had snapped my way through six rolls of film—and according to Getenet, we weren't even anywhere near the *really* good stuff yet!

Technically, the northwest side of the Simien range was one enormous escarpment, the eroded remnant of a vast shield volcano. The buttes and isolated peaks lying beyond it were the hard cores of volcanic outlets from which the surrounding material had worn away. Wherever a crack formed, Pleistocene glaciation and rain had sculptured the highland plateau into a geological wonderland of massive gorges, improbably suspended spurs, yet more sequestered spires and awesome 1000-metre rock faces as sheer as if they'd been sliced with a bread knife.

Getenet was right; the most incredible formations were ours for the viewing over the following three days. Most were well away from the conventional trail which ran between the village of Geech and Chennek, but every vista was worth the extra effort used to reach it.

It continued to cloud over, earlier and earlier each day, so in order to make the most of the marvellous morning light we made camp at night as close to key eyries along the scarp as we could. We spent several hours a day peering through binoculars, scanning each and every grassy ledge on opposing cliff faces in search of Walia ibex, an extremely rare endemic wild goat brought to the verge of extinction at the time of the Italian occupation during

World War II, when hunger forced people into slaughtering them for meat. The encroachment of agriculture continued to limit their habitat and now they were only found within the protected realm of the National Park.

Part of our head scout's daily duty was to record all Walia ibex sightings, noting the size and location of specific herds in a pocket-book. He was remarkably adept at spotting them, but half the time I couldn't make out the long-horned critters from the muted, earthy tones of their precarious hide-outs.

I had better luck espying *ch'elada*[3] or 'bleeding heart' baboons, but then they moved in troops one to six hundred strong. Only a blind, deaf and dumb fool could have missed them.

Our first encounter with the handsome breed was extraordinary. Getenet had brought along a bag of grain to feed to them and in so doing we were able to get very close to a group of some 200 animals. He spread the barley around while Clive, Chris and I lowered ourselves very quietly and slowly to the ground. There was nothing to hide behind; at 4000 metres there was little in the way of vegetation—just the odd lobelia and *ch'elada*-mowed grass.

Getenet stepped back and a couple of male baboons moved in to suss the situation out. They were incredible beasts. The way they walked, with their huge manes blowing in the gentle highland breeze, they looked just like lions stalking out their prey. A large triangle of bare, bright red skin was clearly evident on their chests and their flattened facial features were more like those of monkeys than the classic 'dog snout' of other baboons I'd seen in zoos at home. They were soon joined by their smaller-bodied harems and in less than a minute a bond of trust had been established and a feeding frenzy was well under way.

It was like being in the opening scene of *2001–A Space*

---

[3] *Theropithecus gelada.* 'Gelada' is the Latinised version of the Amharic *ch'elada*.

Odyssey. The noises the *ch'eladas* made as they ate and fought and communicated with each other were disconcerting and strange. They grunted and squealed and screamed like banshees and 'spoke' to each other in harsh, alarmed tones. It was as if we were listening to the first syllables of human language being formed.

When they grew tired of eating, the *ch'eladas* groomed each other, meticulously picking parasites out of their fur. Every now and then a sub-group would start a fight or spook themselves for no reason. The whole troop would suddenly flee, like small children from a wave, crashing with unexpected force onto a shore. When they realised there was no danger, they resumed their positions and continued to eat, nit-pick and chatter.

When they finally decided to leave for good, they threw themselves off the escarpment like a mass of lemmings, seething and bubbling down a vertical series of almost non-existent ledges, as liquid as water tumbling over a fall. Apparently they spent their nights clinging comfortably to the cliff sides and only ventured onto the highland plateau to feed during the day. They must have had secret caves or crevices lined with velcro down there, for I couldn't imagine how they would otherwise adhere themselves to the scarp during sleep.

In order to reach Ras Dejen we had to cross the Mount Bwahit massif, at the far eastern end of the great Simien escarpment. It was one of just a few places where you could descend from the plateau without the aid of ropes. We pounded our way down a trail lined with magnificent flowering red-hot pokers and, wherever the terrain eased on its gradient, through graceful green plots of new barley.

Down in the valley it was hot and dry, the earth starved of colour. I had a sudden inkling of what Ethiopia must be like during a drought, for it dawned on me that none of the cultivated land we'd seen to date had been terraced, negating all possibility for irrigation. When the soil dried out, it would just blow away, for nothing but faith held the topsoil in place. If the rains were too heavy the same problems would ensue.

We crossed the Mesheha[4] River, but Chris and Clive decided a major fossicking session was in order. There were crystals and zebra-stripped lava stones everywhere. I left them to it, and started ascending the other side of the valley alone.

The trail here was lined with cactus and flowering aloe and an hour later when I reached the village of Mizma, I was disheartened to find a thick grove of eucalyptus trees surrounding the houses. I used to get nostalgic whenever I saw eucalypts in the Third World, but now they just made me feel sad.

I don't know who's bright idea it was initially, but giving gums to developing nations had only contributed to—not solved—the earth's environmental woes. Like so many well-intentioned government-funded aid projects afoot in Africa, this Australian-backed one was an embarrassing flop, another monumental Development Folly of our time.

Western aid was too frequently spent on projects designed and implemented by foreign 'experts' who had no real understanding of the African situation. As a result, the entire continent was littered with unwieldy, inappropriate constructions and massive ecological devastation wrought by backfiring or over-ambitious agricultural programs. Over in Ghana there was a Yugoslav mango-canning plant with a capacity greater than the entire world trade in mangoes. In the Sudan a Soviet milk-bottling plant had been idle for nearly thirty years, because, well, Sudanese like to drink their milk fresh from their cows. Colonial British agriculturalists blew $50 million and destroyed vast areas of grazing land in Tanzania before they realised that intensively mechanised groundnuts wouldn't grow and a 'Water-the-Sahara' scheme certainly increased the size of Bedouin camel herds, as it was intended, but in so doing obliterated the scant vegetation of the

---

[4] Also spelt Mayschaha.

region. The environment was unable to support a larger number of animals and all the camels died of starvation, including the original herd.

Without doubt the biggest recent aid disaster in Africa was the village fishponds program around the shores of the 69 500 square-kilometre Lake Victoria. Carnivorous Nile perch were used to stock the back-yard ponds, because they grew from small fry to two-metre monsters in just a couple of years. Unfortunately some escaped into Lake Victoria itself, where the native fish rarely grew over 30 cm in length. The Nile perch population had no competition and quickly exploded.

At first the lake fishermen thought all their Christmases had come at once: they were hauling in much bigger fish more easily than they'd dare imagine. What they didn't know, of course, was that the Nile perch were eating their way through 180 of the 300 different species of fish naturally occurring in the lake.

It was the biggest mass extinction of vertebrates in modern times, but the problems didn't just stop there. The Nile perch was an oilier fish than the native breeds, so fishermen who for centuries had dried their daily catch in the sun took to smoking their large hauls over big charcoal fires. Down came the trees and poof! There went the topsoil. Desertification followed.

Some environmental specialists were now suggesting that since the species which used to eat the algae in the lake were extinct, it was quite possible that an algal bloom would soon cover the surface, absorbing all the oxygen and rendering the entire water-body sterile.

The humble gum story was similarly escalating in its plot, and the problematic consequences, while not quite as dire, were just as irreversible. The eucalyptus tree was chosen by experts as the species best suited to reforest denuded tracts of land all over Africa. It was important to replant something, in order to keep erosion in check and to ensure building materials and firewood for current and future generations. The eucalypt was fast-growing and hardy—but nobody thought to mention it was an abysmal wood for cooking purposes, or that unless you sprayed it with DDT, it was likely to get riddled with termites. Worse than that was its ability to leech the soil of all its nutrients, preventing almost anything from growing thereafter.

Getenet and the horsemen reached Mizma just minutes after I did, and the gem-hunters were not too far behind them. We pitched our camp alongside the village churchyard, and before I had time to get too absorbed in contemplating other aid monstrosities on the continent, evening descended and dinner duty called.

The boys were all craving for a fix of meat, so over a big plate of reconstituted pasta and potato, we agreed to give our horsemen money to buy a sheep from someone in Mizma village the next day. Getenet and our ever-faithful scouts were destined to join us on our mountain climb, but since the Ras Dejen route would find us back in Mizma before nightfall, the horsemen would have the day off. They would be only too delighted to use it preparing a high-protein feast for the 'workers'.

Getting up and down Ras Dejen was made all the more expedient by the thought of a succulent tenderloin of lamb at day's end. We had perfect weather for the climb, and unencumbered by all but the most essential pieces of camera equipment we really flew up and down the peak's bare rocky sides.

Ras Dejen wasn't really a peak, in the true sense of the word—rather a nondescript 'hog-back' on a long undulating ridge-line. Even when we were on the summit, I could not perceive that its height was greater than anything else in the area: we just had to take Getenet's solemn word that the place where we were standing was indeed the highest point on the Horn of Africa.

The lamb roast back at Mizma proved equally disappointing. The meat came from what must have been the oldest sheep in the entire Simien Mountain region—it was tasty, but unfortunately as tough as an old hiking boot to chew. Getenet announced that there was enough for all of us to feast on for at least three days, but we were hardly able to match his enthusiasm and delight. Even Clive would have preferred a date with Tom Cruise to another serving of gristle and stewed leather.

On the last day of our first week on the trail in the Simiens we backtracked to the Mesheha river and crossed a series of massifs which overlooked the foothills of the main escarpment country. On the first ridge we were given a tangle of fresh green peas, plucked straight from a village garden plot. On the second we stopped for lunch, momentarily disturbing a meeting of a hundred local farmers gathered together in a nearby sunfilled field. Getenet said the motley collection of men were members of an assembly, formed to discuss how they could best rehabilitate and develop their land in order to pass on something viable to their children. It was hard to believe—after thousands of years of tilling the soil for feudal land lords and several dozen more doing the same for the government, these people were now actively shaping the agricultural future of their region for themselves.

On the top of the third and final massif, we pulled up at a place called Arkwasiye, nestled on the last pass before the descent route we would take into the lowlands. It had been a long and very hot day on the trail and we reached the quaint Amharic village in no fit state to appreciate its majestic location and charm. We just had enough light and energy left in the day to pitch our tents on the lee-side of the pass.

When we woke the next morning our camp was surrounded by inquisitive children who had never seen white people before. They were so natural and unaffected; they stroked the back of my hand and planted little kisses on my knuckles, rested their heads against my knees and took turns at climbing into my lap for a cuddle. It was so beautiful, I think I could have spent the rest of my life there. As it was I didn't move for several hours, playing a bunch of different games and using them to further my attempt at learning the rudiments of the Amharic language.

People from all over the surrounding countryside were heading for Arkwasiye's regular Saturday market and those coming from the northern lowlands or western highlands filed straight past our itinerant camp. Their dumbfounded stares suggested they themselves had had little or no contact with foreigners and before long we were the talk of the village. There was almost as big a crowd on the top of the pass looking down on us as there was buying and trading goods in the open-air market on the other side of the saddle-shaped pass.

I couldn't leave the kids alone, nor they me, so we all wandered down into the thick of the market action together. Chris was busy filming—and Clive photographing—a lone lammergeyer, soaring directly over the camp. Getenet had seen it in the distance half an hour beforehand, and had placed our sheep-stew bones on a nearby rock, hoping to attract it close enough for the budding cameramen to shoot. The giant bird of prey had a wingspan nearly two metres wide, and standing it was probably only marginally shorter than Getenet himself, so the boys were pretty wrapt in the frame-filling images they were recording. When it started swooping down to grab and smash the bones they went into an absolute frenzy. It would have been easier to prise one of the spare ribs from the lammergeyer than it was to persuade either of the guys to join me 'downtown'.

Within seconds of entering the open-market *melée*, I was completely swamped by people. Toothless old women were grabbing onto me, cupping my face in their hands and planting kisses on my cheeks. Men were reaching out to shake my hand and the kids accompanying me looked as if they'd just won some fabulous trophy in a footy match. I was buoyed by the crowd, carried by their waves of curiosity and affection. I drifted through a sea of dried chillies, used clothing, crudely fashioned clay pots, wizened medicinal roots and herbs, surplus barley, maize, basket grasses, hand-woven cloth, potatoes, chickens and donkeys.

Just when I thought I was about to drown in the spectacle,

Getenet and Chris appeared and threw me a much-needed lifeline. The village chief wanted us to pay his family a visit. We couldn't find Clive—he had finished photographing the lammergeyer and we assumed he was somewhere in the market, refocusing his attentions, but we couldn't actually see him anywhere.

Four women were inside the headman's kitchen hut, preparing a pot of strong black coffee: his mother, his wife and two of her girlfriends. The light from the fire burning in the hearth was warm and glowing and their faces shone like burnished bronze. They smiled as we entered, and motioned for us to sit on a raised earthen platform covered in a half-dozen crusty old hides.

The chief's wife placed a small shot-glass of pure black caffeine in my hand. I looked up to thank her and noticed her neck was covered in a tattoo resembling an elaborate six-tiered choker. It clearly marked her as a married woman. A silver Coptic cross on a black ribbon hung over the tattoo and her hair was braided in a multitude of tiny plaits anchored to her scalp. She was so beautiful, I was lost for words. Chris's jaw fell with an audible 'clunk' to the floor.

We talked to the headman through Getenet, mostly about returning to his village to film it for our proposed documentary series. I was just considering broaching the subject of taking up permanent residency when our trusty little guide suggested it was time we packed up and pushed off down the road. It was midday already and the scouts were getting restless.

I don't think a place or a group of people in Africa touched me more than Arkwasiye and its residents. Their trust, their uninhibited acceptance, were a gift I would cherish forever.

In that tiny, otherwise insignificant village, I came to realise again, as I had in Uganda, why this whole sad and sorry continent endured. While we in the West despaired for Africa and looked at it only in terms of its overwhelming past failings, Africa itself chose to rejoice in its unknowable future. Our pessimism, no matter how realistic a point of view it seemed, was no match at all for the optimism of the masses at ground level.

After decades dominated by starvation and dictatorship, the people of Arkwasiye were not defeated, as one might expect— they were full of ambition and faith. Hope was the light at the end of not only their tunnel, but that of Africa's Horn absolutely, and even though history and fate had conspired to extinguish it many times over, it refused to go out completely.

Hope was the light of the entire world, but until that morning in Arkwasiye, I was blind to this truth. I had searched much of Africa, trying to find the secret of its resolution in a sunrise; trying to solve the riddle of its purpose with a landscape.

Until that morning in Arkwasiye, I had not even thought to seek the answer from within. I had not thought to look for it inside the very people I had spent my life pitying, so when I found it shining there, inside their rheumy eyes, my own completely clouded over with tears.

As we were leaving, the chief presented us with a chicken. I felt empty-handed, with nothing to give him in return. I had not come to Ethiopia expecting to receive such presents, and putting my hand in my pocket seemed a wholly inappropriate gesture. That was what I had done for years, in response to disaster and tragedy; it was not something I could therefore do now out of thanks or even in friendship. All I could give the chief was a smile, and the silent promise to share that chicken, that gift of hope from mother Africa, with all the people of my own troubled world.

We waved our last goodbyes, turned, and ran down the lee-side of the Arkwasiye saddle. I felt weightless, as if I could fly, as if I were a kite on a breeze. The 'dark' continent was shining, and once again, I was witness to wonder.

EPILOGUE

THE LAST WEEK of our adventure in Ethiopia flew by in a miraculous blur. We trekked through the countryside in awe, one moment marvelling at delicate lace curtains of light in the forest, the next swallowed by shadows cast down from the great escarpment wall. It was rough going, following the lay of the land which, unlike that of the highland terrain, impeded direct travel from one point to the next.

We returned to Nairobi, and Chris and I flew west to scale Mount Cameroon. That was OK—if a little wet—but my heart was no longer tied to the challenge of climbing, so I derived little pleasure from the experience.

The real goal of our journey, as far as I was concerned, had been realised in the village of Arkwasiye. I had left a piece of my heart up there, as big as any I had given to my precious Himalaya.

I had found the timeless soul of Africa in her people, and in so doing, had become a loose thread in their tapestry. I too, for however brief a moment, had been a part of the majesty co-eternal. A part of the beginning, the end and the everything . . .